The Qur'an is "a guidance for mankind… and the distinction (between right and wrong)". Qur'an 2:185

Have they never learned to think for themselves?
God has not created the heavens and the earth and all that is between them without [an inner] truth and a term set [by Him]: (30:8)

"We will show them Our Signs <u>in the farthest reaches of the universe</u> and *within their own souls…*" (41: 53)

© 2022 Viverealtrimenti Ltd, London
ISBN 978-1-9996689-4-5
The calligram on the cover is the work of Amjed Rifaie:
www.amjedrifaie.com

www.viverealtrimenti.com

İbrahim Özdemir

Care for Creation
An Islamic Perspective

About the Author

İbrahim Özdemir is a professor of philosophy at Uskudar University, Istanbul, Turkey.

His major is environmental philosophy and ethics; his academic interests include environmental philosophy and ethics, ecology and religion, practical ethics, philosophical counseling, critical thinking, and Islamic philosophy.

He was member of the drafting team of the *Islamic Declaration for Global Climate Change* (2015):
https://unfccc.int/news/islamic-declaration-on-climate-change.

Presently, he was assigned as member of core and draft team to write and finalize *Al-Mizan: A Covenant for the Earth* to be presented to UN:
https://www.unep.org/al-mizan-covenant-earth.
His books include

Rumî and Confucius on Meaning of Life, Amazon, New Jersey, 2020;
The Ethical Dimension of Human Attitude Towards Nature, second edition, Insan Publications, Istanbul, 2008;
Globalization, Ethics and Islam, Ian Markham and İbrahim Özdemir, Aldershot, Ashgate. 2005.

Contact information:
E-mail: ib60dmr@gmail.com
Web: https://ibrahimozdemir.web.tr/
LinkedIn: https://www.linkedin.com/in/ib60dmr/
Academia: https://abo.academia.edu/IbrahimOzdemir

Contents

Forword	9
Preface	15
Introduction	17
1.1. What is the Environment?	23
1.2. The Problem	25
1.3. Think about the Future and Get Prepared!	29
2. The Islamic View of the Environment	33
3. The Importance of Cleanliness	41
4. The Cleanliness of the Social Environment	45
5. The Preservation of Trees, Woodland And Green Areas	47
5.1. Trees in the Qur'an	47

5.2. Trees and Woodlands in Hadiths of the Prophet (PBUH)	50
6. The Protection of Animals	53
6.1. Animals in the Qur'an	54
6.2. Animals in Hadiths of the Prophet (PBUH)	55
7. Some Examples From Islamic History	61
8. Not Wasting the Earth's Resources	67
APPENDIX 1	75
APPENDIX 2	91
Bibliography and Further Readings	113

Forword

«We are facing a global emergency. Our scientists tell us that human-induced climate change brought on by the burning of fossil fuels has taken the human race and our fellow species into the sixth mass extinction event of life on Earth»[1].

This is the alarming warning at the beginning of Jeremy Rifkin's book *The Green New Deal* but the main purpose of the author — a well-reputed scholar who wrote over twenty books about the impact of scientific and technological changes on the economy, the workforce, society, and the environment — is to be constructive, more than simply critical, concretely encouraging the transition to a more sustainable world. In fact, he proceeds to present a rich amount of data showing how "**within the next eight years, solar and wind will be far cheaper than fossil fuel energies, forcing a showdown with the fossil fuel energy**".

It may be early to confirm whether we are prepared for a transnational *Green New Deal*. However, it is both clear the planet could survive this critical period and that everybody should be willing to contribute!

In other words: there is no time to waste complaining and fearing an imminent catastrophe; we must all do our best to promote a paradigm shift. It is a shared duty!

Muslims, all over the world and more than other people, are compelled to contribute to implementing a Green New Deal.

---

[1] Jeremy Rifkin, *The Green New Deal*, 2019, p. 1.

It is well known that Islam is the fastest growing religion today, with around 1.8 billion people.

Therefore, a greater engagement within Muslim organizations focusing on and addressing environmental issues will have relevant implications.

Doing research on "Green Islam", as a member of the Green team of the *Muslim Council of Britain*, I found online and then met in person (in Bologna — Italy — in October 2021) Professor İbrahim Özdemir. More precisely, I have initially found his article with Al Jazeera[2], where he claimed that:

«Many Muslim majority countries bear the brunt of climate change, but their cultural awareness of it and climate action are often staggeringly limited. A movement of Islamic environmentalism based on Islamic tradition — rather than imported white saviour environmentalism based on first-world political campaigns — can address both».

Indeed the relationship between Islam and ecology is more profound than the average person can guess.

Nowadays, this issue is still poorly discussed. Still, we can easily affirm, following authors such as Seyyed Hossein Nasr, Ibrahim Abdul Matin, Fazlun Khalid, and İbrahim Özdemir himself, that Islam is a genetically environmentalist religion!

We have not to forget — as Abdul Matin highlights in his book *Green Deen: What Islam Teaches About Protecting The Planet* — that one of the fundamental principles of Islam is *Mizan*: balance; a general concept including, of course, the duty to find a virtuous balance with the environment surrounding

---

[2] You can read the full article here:
https://www.aljazeera.com/opinions/2020/8/12/what-does-islam-say-about-climate-change-and-climate-action.

and supporting us with whatever we need to survive and, potentially, to have a pleasant life. That is to say: with God's creation.

«In the name of God, the Gracious, the Merciful.
The Compassionate. Has taught the Quran. He created man. And taught him clear expression. The sun and the moon move *according to plan*. And the stars and the trees prostrate themselves. And the sky, He raised, and He set up *the balance*. So do not transgress in *the balance*. But maintain the weights with *justice*, and do not violate *the balance*».

(The Holy Quran, 55:1-9)

It is evident from the above discussion that justice and balance are universal laws [of God] and that (as a result) humans should conduct a just and balanced life.

When we reflect on the moral implications of these verses, we will see that these verses alone would be enough for developing an environmental ethic and sustainability from the Qur'an itself.

First, justice and balance are universal; second, this universal balance is created and sustained by God, and third, humans must both attempt to comprehend this universal balance.

Therefore, to achieve a virtuous balance between man and the environment, some Islamic theorists and organizations are constantly working to stem the harmful effects of climate change, inaugurating a global Green New Deal.

To give some practical examples, in 2015 it has been, drafted *The Islamic Declaration on Global Climate Change* fully reported in the Appendix.

Two members of the Islamic Declaration Team — Professor İbrahim Özdemir and the Sri Lankan Scholar living in the UK, Fazlun Khalid — are also involved in the international project (supervised by UNEP) *Al-Mizan: A Covenant for the Earth*.

Quoting from the respective website[3]:

«*Al-Mizan: A Covenant for the Earth* presents an Islamic outlook of the environment in a bid to strengthen local, regional, and international actions that combat climate change and other threats to the planet. It is a global endeavour to engage Islamic scholars and Muslim institutions in developing and adopting this Call.
Al-Mizan: A Covenant for the Earth is a restatement of the principles governing the protection of nature in a form that meets current challenges. It examines the ethics behind the social patterning of human existence. It enquires into how they could be brought to life today, working in harmony with the heartbeat of the natural world.
Environmentalism is deeply embedded in the veins of Islam.

It is about personal behaviour and how it manifests in our association with others. It is also about being considerate in our relationship with the natural world and other sentient beings.

These principles grew from the foundations established by Prophet Muhammad into a range of rules and institutions that manifested an expression of a genuinely holistic life. It was based on the Qur'an, and it could be distilled into three categories, namely encouraging public good, forbidding the wrong action, and acting in moderation at all times:

"Let there be a community among you that calls for what is good, urges what is right and forbids what is wrong, they are the ones who have success"

(The Holy Quran, 3: 104)».

There are also numerous Islamic organizations at the international level constantly engaged in safeguarding the environment.
We can offer here a short list including only a fraction of them:

---

[3] *https://www.unep.org/al-mizan-covenant-earth*

Green Muslims: A volunteer-driven headquartered in metropolitan Washington, DC, working to connect Muslims everywhere to nature and environmental activism.
They host educational, service, and outdoor recreational events and strive to serve as a bridge connecting the Muslim community with local climate action organizations.

Muslim Global Relief: Awarded the UK's Best Charity of 2018 at the National British Muslim Awards and finalist for 2019. MGR works in remote villages across Ghana, Indonesia, Pakistan, Gambia, India, and Palestine. MGR brings them sustainable development solutions through the Big Muslim Fund, such as safe water, planting fruit trees, and sponsorship of orphan education.

Muslim Hands: An international aid agency and NGO working in over thirty countries worldwide, with projects prioritizing environmental sustainability.

Khaleafa: A "sacred trust" based in Canada whose goal is to reignite the discourse surrounding the Islamic approach to environmentalism and draw upon these teachings' essence.

Wisdom in Nature: A UK-based network offering team training in Inclusive Leadership and Facilitation, Permaculture, and Islamic Ecology.

Green Prophet: Headquartered in Ontario, Canada, with satellite offices in Amman and Tel Aviv, the Green Prophet is a trusted source for green design, architecture, lifestyle, policy, and renewable energy news in the Middle East.
It was founded by biologist, journalist, and technology entrepreneur Karin Kloosterman, whose work and commentary have appeared on major international media, such as Bloom-

berg, Discovery Channel, CNN, The Washington Post, Al Jazeera, and many more platforms.

The Eco-Muslim: It is part of Zaufishan Iqbal's "eco-jihad," a greener effort to ensure our community is cleaner than before. Zaufishan encourages everyone to live on less by following the 4Rs: Reuse! (e.g., leftover water) Reduce! (How much food you waste) Recycle! (Your unwanted clothes) Reject! (Poverty, homelessness, and exploitation) Insha-Allah (God willing)".

In conclusion, we can comfortably say the Muslim world is, in several ways, "caring about creation," but, of course, due to the dramatic complexity of the actual lack of balance (*Mizan*) between *Man and Nature* (to quote the title of a crucial book on the relation between Islam and ecology, authored by Seyyed Hossein Nasr), a lot of extra work should be quickly done.

Professor Özdemir in one of the most active environmentamentalists worldwide, that's why I'm honoured to support him in publishing this book with the hope his theoretical effort will inspire several new concrete initiatives to protect our wonderful environment, flora, and fauna, the stupendous creation that God has deliberately entrusted to us.

Indeed he gave us, as we will see in the following pages, the role of *Khalifa*: protectors of nature, a gift we should never betray!

I definitely wish you a pleasant and inspirational reading!

Manuel Olivares
www.viverealtrimenti.com

Preface

The Greek Philosopher Plato (428 – 348 BC) wonders over the beauty in nature and dare to ask what is the source of this beauty. Asking this question, his philosophical journey started. Then, he discovered that the source of the beauty we observe in nature is beyond what is visible.

Muslim Sufi masters, with the guidance of the Qur'an, see all beauty in heavens and on the earth as a reflection of Divine beauty. For example, Al-Nablusi (d.1731), a Sufi poet of the 18th century of Damascus invites us to see and read the whole universe as a book:

«Reflect upon the lines of the [Book of the] Universe,
for they are letters to you from the highest realm».

Our spiritual masters were sure that *"the Book of creation displays orderliness as clearly as the midday sun and exhibits the power's miracle in every word or letter"*.

The Qur'an, therefore, unceasingly addresses the human mind and heart so that it heightens his/her feelings and emotions and make him/her behold and contemplate the wonders of the Universe as if we see them for the first time.

The physical world is full of beautiful mysteries and awe-inspiring events that have captivated many eyes and fascinated many hearts. So, we can ask ourselves what is the source of the Maldives beautiful coral reefs and marine ecology some of the most spectacular in the world, attracting millions of visitors from different destinations?

Let me remind you how the first chapter of the Qur'an, *al-Fatiha* (the Opening) presents both Allah and the universe to us: "*ALL PRAISE is due to God alone, the Sustainer of all the worlds*". In this instance, the term *worlds* denotes all categories of existence both in the physical and the spiritual sense.

Moreover, the Arabic word *rabbī l-'ālamīn* — that we can render as *Sustainer* — embraces a wide complex of meanings not easily expressed by a single term in another language.

It comprises the ideas of having a just claim to the possession of anything and, consequently, authority over it, as well as of rearing, sustaining and fostering anything from its inception to its completion.

Thus, the head of a family is called *rabb ad-dar* (master of the house) because he has authority over it and is responsible for its maintenance; similarly, his wife is called *rabbat ad-dar* (mistress of the house). Preceded by the definite article *al*, the designation *rabb* is applied, in the Qur'an, exclusively to Allah as the sole fosterer and sustainer of all creation — objective as well as conceptual — and therefore the ultimate source of all authority. (Asad, 1: 2)

So, we can ask ourselves what is the source of the Maldives beautiful coral reefs and marine ecology; some of the most spectacular in the world, attracting millions of visitors from different destinations?

Most importantly, how can we protect these beauties for the future generation? In other words, it is a moral imperative to ask ourselves how we can meet the needs of the present without compromising the ability of future generations to meet their own needs.

This small booklet has been translated into different languages and published in different countries.

I do hope that this small booklet can help you look at the environment encompassing us from a new and fresh perspective based on revealed knowledge.

İbrahim Özdemir; Istanbul, 2022.

Introduction

An international conference was held in Chicago from 11th to 13th November 1997 to which representatives of all the major religions had been invited, and in which I myself also took part. In the course of it we were asked to note down what we considered to be the three most important problems facing the world.

When the results were compiled, the following emerged as the most important problems:

1- Peace.
2- Environmental problems.
3- Education.

A decision was taken by the members of all the different religions participating in the conference to cooperate in solving these problems. For it has been stated by social scientists that moral and religious values will dominate the 21st century.

In the present booklet, which I have prepared in this spirit, I have attempted to put forward the Islamic principles concerning the environment.

My aim has been to set out clearly how Muslims consider the environment, or how they should consider it.

If this small work assists in the growth of environmental consciousness, all humanity will profit from it. For the environment belongs to all of us. Or more correctly, it has been given to all of us in trust by Allah.

Our greatest responsibility should therefore be to treat this trust in the best way, and not to pollute it or destroy it.

Furthermore, those things that have to be done, have to be

done here and now; we must put nothing off until tomorrow.

Success is from Allah alone.
İbrahim ÖZDEMİR

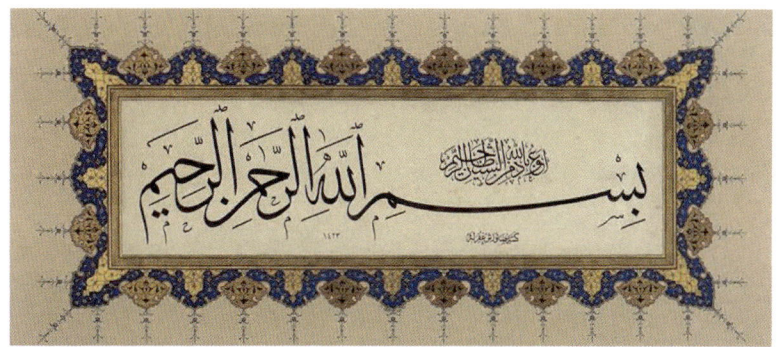

In the Name of God — the Most Compassionate, Most Merciful.
We too offer the praise and thanks and gifts that all animate creatures offer through the tongues of their beings and lives to their Creator, the Lord of all worlds, Who said:

«If you tried to count God's blessings, you would never be able to number them». (Qur'an 16:18)

Never-ending blessings and peace be upon the Prophet Mercy to all creation, who said: *"I came to perfect morality"*. *('Ajluni, Kashf al-Khafa, i, 211).*

He also declared that "An important reason for my being sent to mankind by Almighty God was to perfect good conduct and morality and deliver mankind from immorality and vice."

All creatures say Bismillah and act in the name of Almighty God.
Basmala, *"In the name of God, the most gracious, the merciful"* occurred 114 times in the Quran. Therefore, *Bismillah*, "**In the Name of God,**" is the start of all things good.

This short and poetic phrase contains the true essence of the Quran.

The common translation of this phrase, however, fails to capture the *true depth of meaning* or *the inspirational message of this beautiful expression*.

The phrase "*In the name of*" *(Bismi)* is an idiom having the connotation of *with the blessings of, under the governance of, as an instrument of, as a representative of, on behalf of, with the support of,* or *for the glory of.* In each of these cases, the expression "*In the name of*" indicates that one is submitting to, honoring or glorifying that which is referred to.

The central idea here is that whatever we do, every step that we take, every breath that we breathe is done for, because of, and through the essence of the One *who has created us.*

Therefore, *Bismillah* is cited in daily prayers and other contexts by Muslims. Meanwhile, all Islamic books, theological, philosophical, and poetic whatever genre they belong, start with *Bismillah…*

Accordingly, a Muslim believes that *all creatures act in the name of Almighty God.*

«All trees say: "In the Name of God," fill their hands from the treasury of mercy, and offer them to us.
All gardens say: "In the Name of God" and become cauldrons from the kitchens of Divine power in which are cooked numerous varieties of different foods.
All blessed animals like cows, camels, sheep, and goats, say: "In the Name of Allah," and produce springs of milk from the abundance of mercy, offering us a most delicate and pure food like the water of life in the name of the Provider». (Nursi, 1998).

Briefly, this blessed phrase is a mark of Islam and also forms and shapes our perception of God, the universe, and ourselves.

Most certainly, mercy such as this requires universal and sincere thanks, earnest and genuine respect.

The Manuscript of the book *Marvels of Creatures and the Strange Things Existing* by Zakariya Qazvini (1203–1283).
The first page starts with *Basmala* and the praise of Allah "All praise is due to God, Who created *Marvels of Creatures* with His Power and designed *Strange Things Existing* with His Wisdom".

1.1. What is the Environment?

We know that the problem of the environment is one of the most serious of our times. It threatens not only us, but the whole world, the future generations and their right to live in a healthy environment. It is, therefore, a great source of anxiety for contemporary humanity.

This compels us to understand the environmental problems and to help in solving them. We should therefore first of all ask: *what do we understand by 'the environment'?* That is, *what is the environment?*

One scientist answered this question by saying *"we have 4095 environments"*. By this he wanted to emphasize that when saying "environment," it is insufficient to understand only the natural environment.

As a Muslim, I understand the phrase "Sustainer of All the Worlds" (that is to say: the "Sustainer of all environments" or: "Who embraces and encompasses all environments") as having exactly the same meaning.

The Qur'an expresses this truth as follows:

«To God belong the East and the West; whithersoever you turn, there is God's countenance. For God is All-Embracing, All-Knowing».

(Qur'an, 2:115)

Another noteworthy point of the Qur'an's related to the environment is this:

«In the Name of God, the Merciful, the Compassionate.
All praise be to God, the Sustainer of all the worlds».

(Qur'an, 1: 1-2)

This induces us to consider the environment from a broad perspective. In fact, such broad, inclusive, and awesome definition of environment can be seen in the works of makers of Islamic civilization.

Al-Ghazali (d.1111.) when praised God joins the cosmic prayer of all beings the following eloquent and beautiful words:

«Countless gratitude equal to the number of stars in the sky, drops in the rainfalls, leaves of the trees, particles of sand of deserts, the atoms in the heavens and the earth is befitting only for God, Whose attribute is His Oneness and All Majesty, Greatness, Highness, and Excellence is specific for Him».
(al-Ghazali, 2019)

Therefore, we should not forget that the Creator and Owner of all environments is at the same time our Creator.

Thus, our environment is formed by *our house, garden, and car, the air we breathe, the water we drink, the town in which we live, and the people we live with*. So too, it is formed by the seas, lakes, rivers, roads, mountains, and forests, which are shared by all the members of society.

Thus, when we say "environment," we understand all-natural surroundings in which we and all living creatures live. While by "environmental pollution," we mean the dirtying and spoiling of these natural surroundings.

The air is polluted, the seas are polluted, the ozone layer is diminishing, animal species are becoming extinct.

Pollution of *the social environment* should be added to these: poverty, deprivation, homelessness, migration problems, racialism, abandoned children, drug abuse, alcohol addiction, and other problems.

Let`s look at the problem in some details and see what has been happening in around us.

1.2. The Problem

Environmental problems in general and climate change, in particular, are frightening all humanity and the very existence of life on earth.

Jared Diamond is an academic physiologist and ecologist, with overlays of evolutionary biology, environmental science, and social sciences.

His book *Collapse: How Societies Choose to Fail or Succeed* (published in 2005) casts light on some of today's emerging large-scale environmental problems and their overreaching and overwhelming impact on societies: the risks from global climate change, degradation of arable land, fisheries depletion, widespread freshwater shortages, and losses of species and ecosystems.

Furthermore, the book tackles a big question: Why, when facing environmental decline, do some societies succeed while others fail? (Diamond 2005, 487-495).

Jared Diamond's previous book *Guns, Germs and Steel* (published in 1997) argued that some societies became more powerful, wealthy, and dominant because of fortuitous circumstances: geography, natural resources (especially plant and animal species), and the diffusion of Technologies (Diamond, 1997).

Collapse, however, explores why some societies have failed to achieve sustainable management of their resource base and their social structures. Diamond, as a result of painstaking extensive research, poses important, contemporary questions and seeks answers in the spirit of multidisciplinary terms.

Diamond's academic background helps him to present instructive contrasts; for example, in *Collapse* between Vikings in Greenland during the slightly warmer Middle Ages (cultural rigidity, marginal environmental assets, and an inability to cope with a changing climate as cooling beset 14th century Europe).

He presents us with some other examples in support of his argument. Relying on his chosen historical examples

Diamond posits five factors that influence the fate of such societies: *the extent of environmental degradation; changes in climatic conditions; the hostility and power of neighbors; support from trading with friendly neighbors; and internal power relations, governance, and decision-making capacity* (Diamond, 2005; italic added).

On the other hand, he explores the counterfactual question, too: Do societies that do well on these criteria avoid decline when faced with environmental degradation of their own making?

He, relying on examples of the South-west Pacific islanders of Tikopia, New Guinea highlanders, and Tokugawa Japan argues that "a combination of cultural flexibility, accrued and applied wisdom and acceptance of the need for restraint have enabled alleviation of situations of ecological vulnerability" (Diamond, ibid).

This also summarizes the main thesis of this paper that is if we can learn from history in general and environmental history in particular with a spirit of multidisciplinary, then we can learn from the past and propose more creative and meaningful solutions to the problems we have been facing today.

According to a report by *the Intergovernmental Panel on Climate Change* (IPCC), leading climate scientists now feel confident that human activity is heating the planet since the Industrial Revolution.

Therefore, environmental problems and climate change mitigates adaptation and requires not only technical solutions but also *better insights in the understanding of relevant belief and identity systems*, in which religion and culture play an important role.

Human attitudes, convictions, and ultimately our consumption patterns will play an important role in our environment and climate adaptation and mitigation.

Religion and culture, therefore, are the key determinant of individual convictions and a central marker of behavior and community belonging.

Therefore, critical action is needed by our leaders, scholars, scientists, as well as NGO`s to address urgent, pending, and increasing environmental degradation, and related challenges of social and economic unsustainability in their respective countries. Thus, we can envisage a world in which our children and grandchildren may enjoy an equal, just, inclusive, and sustainable economic growth and decent work for all.

It will also secure the future of our countries, which by 2050 will be more crowded than now by regulating consumption and production patterns and use of all-natural resources — from air to land, from deserts to forests, from rivers, lakes, and aquifers to oceans and seas and from frozen tundra to expanding towns and cities — with *a spirit of sustainability,* which *"meets the needs of the present without compromising the ability of future generations to meet their own needs"*.

Therefore, UNEP and UNESCO concluded that these problems cannot be solved by merely applying scientific and technological tools.

We need new instruments to mobilize people toward a common cause. Then they began to emphasize that religion and culture can significantly address climate change, biodiversity loss, pollution, deforestation, desertification, unsustainable land and water use, and other urgent issues identified in a shared vision by all nations in line with *the 2030 Agenda for Sustainable Development.*

Many contemporary thinkers and scientists for example? have stated that religion has an important role to play in overcoming these problems and in the development of comprehensive and integral environmental consciousness.

Moreover, environmental, social, and economic threats are aimed at everyone without discrimination, whether Christian, Jew, Hindu, Buddhist, Muslim, and secular. Therefore, we have to cooperate and join our energies for a better future.

As the threat is common, the response must be common.

This will empower the spirit of solidarity and cooperation in our respective societies.

However, I will present my findings from the Qur'an, the Prophet Muhammad's (PBUH) teachings (Sunnah), and Islamic culture on positive attitudes and behaviors to the environment, climate change, and sustainable development.

I will argue that Islamic values regarding environment "over the centuries have been elaborated upon by a succession of mystics, scholars, jurists, and teachers responding to real problems experienced by the growing community of Muslims in various parts of the world. (Khalid, 2019).

Therefore, I will suggest at the end of this talk that we need a sound and comprehensive strategy for the environment, climate change, sustainable development, population movements, and even the transfer of technologies.

The freedom, dignity, moral and economic well-being of the future generations also depends on the decision and steps we will take today. Otherwise, all beauties bestowed upon us by God and attracts each year millions of tourists to the Maldives and the traditional eco-friendly Maldivian way of life would cease, and we will leave a troubled world to generation next.

I will argue that to care for environmental protection, ocean ecosystems, and coral reefs and to preserve the islands and their surrounding habitat must be a religious and moral imperative for each of us. We have to think about the future now and today.

We have to ask ourselves in the face of shreds of evidence provided by scientists if we are ready or not to make sacrifices for our grandchildren and leave a better and brighter world then we found it.

1.3. Think about the Future and Get Prepared!

Outlining the challenges threatening our present and future life, we have to get ready respond to these challenges in due time. The Qur'an warns and guides people to think about the future:

«O you who have attained to faith! Remain conscious of God; and let every human being look to what he sends ahead for the morrow!».

(Qur'an, 59:18)

Moroccan scholar and diplomat Mahdi Elmandjra (1990: 2-3) reflections on verses regarding the future have important messages for us: all these verses from the Quran call us to make *the best possible use of the present and to carefully and intelligently prepare for the future*; the future meaning the rest of our life on earth and the hereafter... [the Quran] recommend[s] that we make projections and work out different options in order to enhance our ability to cope with the requirements of the future and to improve our well-being. *The Islamic Declaration on Global Climate Change*[4], which was prepared by a group of Muslim Environmentalist in August 2015, was a wake-up call to Muslims around the globe.

---

[4] The full text of *The Islamic Declaration on Global Climate Change* is in the Appendix.

The Declaration was written by an international group of Islamic scholars, with a vision to draw on Islamic sources and ancient tradition to provide solutions to the modern crisis of climate change.

The Declaration incorporates this excerpt from the Quran:

«Corruption has appeared on land and sea. Because of what people's own hands have wrought, so that they may taste something of what they have done; so that hopefully they will turn back»

(Qur'an, 30:41)

Based on this, the Declaration states:

«We recognize the corruption (fasad) that humans have caused on the Earth due to our relentless pursuit of economic growth and consumption. Its consequences have been--
Global climate change, which is our present concern, in addition to:
-Contamination and befoulment of the atmosphere, land, inland water systems, and seas;
-Soil erosion, deforestation, and desertification;
-Destruction, degradation, and fragmentation of the habitats of the earth's communities of life, with the devastation of some of the most biologically diverse and productive ecosystems such as rainforests, freshwater wetlands, and coral reefs;
-Impairment of ecosystem benefits and services;
-Introduction of invasive alien species and genetically modified organisms;

-Damage to human health, including a host of modern-day diseases».

Notably, the Declaration also states:

«We call on the people of all nations and their leaders to...Realize

that to chase after unlimited economic growth in a planet that is finite and already overloaded is not viable. Growth must be pursued wisely and in moderation.
[…]
We call upon corporations, finance, and the business sector to change from the current business model which is based on an unsustainable escalating economy, and to adopt a circular economy that is wholly sustainable».

Therefore, the future should be approached in a pluralistic manner (futures) thus leaving open a wide range of options.

Islam is a faith and a way of life. It is also an exploratory vision of life on earth and in the hereafter. It is our outlooks that determine our deeds for which we are answerable to ourselves, to society and to God.

In Islam Man, whatever he does, is mindful of the impact of his action on the rest of his life as well as on his fate in the Last Judgment (Elmandjra 1990, 1-2).

2. The Islamic View of the Environment

In Islam, everything in the universe is created by God. It is God Who adorns the skies with the sun, the moon and the stars, and the face of the earth with flowers, trees, gardens, orchards, and the various animal species.

It is again God Who causes the rivers and streams to flow on the earth, Who upholds the skies (without support), causes the rain to fall, and places the boundary between night and day.

The universe together with all its richness and vitality is the work and art of God, that is, of the Creator. It is again God Who creates all plants and animals as pairs, in this way causing their procreation. God created man subsequently to all these.

We are God's vicegerents on the earth; it has been given us in trust. Just as we are not the lords of nature and the world, so the world is not our property which we can dispose of as we wish or as we are able. God created nature and it belongs to God. Everything in nature is a sign of God's existence; that is, a token or missive. The Qur'an expresses this truth as follows:

«We shall show them our signs in the [furthest] regions [of the earth], and in their own souls».

(Qur'an, 41:53)

«Behold! In the creation of the heavens and the earth; in the alternation of the night and the day; in the sailing of the ships through the ocean for the profit of mankind; in the rain which God sends down from the skies, and the life which He gives therewith to an earth that is dead; in the beasts of all kinds that He scatters through the earth; in the change of the winds, and the clouds subjugated between the sky and earth — [here] indeed are signs for a people who thinks».

(Qur'an, 2:164)

This verse illustrates why Muslim scholars look on nature as a book, even calling it *"the book of the universe."* Thus, just like the Qur'an, the universe makes known to us our *Sustainer and Creator*. And the book of the universe has been entrusted to us to preserve and protect.

Should those who hold the Qur'an in respect and awe, not touching it unless purified by ablutions, not also treat the book of the universe respectfully and lovingly?

Our duty, therefore, as God's vicegerents and trustees, is to show respect for the trust, and to preserve it carefully, in no way wasting its natural resources when using or consuming them.

«And you certainly know already the first form of creation: why then do you not celebrate His praises?
See you the seed that you sow in the ground?
Is it you that cause it to grow, or are We the cause?
Were it our will, We could crumble it to dry powder, and you would be left in wonderment,
[Saying], "We are indeed left with debts [for nothing];
"Indeed are we shut out [of the fruits of our labour]."
See you the water which you drink?
Do you bring it down [in rain] from the cloud or do We?
Were it our will, We could make it salt [and unpalatable]; then why do you not give thanks?
See you the fire which you kindle?
Is it you who grow the tree which feeds the fire, or do We grow it?
It is We Who make it a means to remind [you of Us], and an article of comfort and convenience for the denizens of deserts.
Then celebrate with praises the name of your Sustainer, the Supreme!». (Qur'an, 56:62-74)

As the final Divine message, Islam insistently draws our attention to this sacred and spiritual dimension of nature.

It teaches us too that we are created by God and that we shall return to Him in order to give account for our actions.

This means that we are answerable for all that we do, both the good, and the evil.

As God's vicegerent on earth, at the Last Judgement man will be called to account for how he acted towards the trust, and how he treated it.

«So, glory to Him in Whose hands is the dominion of all things: Ant to Him will you be all brought back...».

(Qur'an: 36: 83)

According to Yusuf Ali the message conveyed in this verse is the core of Revelation; it explains the Hereafter: All things were created by God; are maintained by Him; and will go back to Him. But the point of special interest to man is that man will also be brought back to God and is answerable to Him, and to Him alone.

The concept of Divine unity is the basis and essence of Islam.

Divine unity is apparent in the unity of humanity and of nature.

God's vicegerents on the earth, the holders of His trust, are therefore primarily responsible for preserving the unity of creatures, the integral wholeness of the world, the flora and fauna, and wildlife and natural environment.

Thus, 'unity', 'trust', and 'responsibility' are the three basic concepts of Islam.

These principles are at the same time the chief pillars of the Islamic environmental ethic.

They form also the fundamental values taught by the Qur'an.

When we read the Qur'an's verses about the earth, we find that they suggest strongly that it is for man a peaceful place which he should take heed of.

Thus, the Qur'an draws our attention to nature and to the events that occur in it:

«The seven heavens and the earth, and all beings therein, declare His glory; there is not a thing but celebrates His praise; and yet you understand not how they declare His glory! Verily He is Oft-Forbearing, Most Forgiving!». (Qur'an, 17:44. See also, 57:1; 62:1)

«See you not that to God bow down in worship all things that are in the heavens and on earth — the sun, the moon, the stars; the hills, the trees, the animals; and a great number of mankind?».

(Qur'an, 22:18)

«And do We not send down from the clouds water in abundance,
That We may produce therewith corn and vegetables,
And gardens of luxurious growth?».

(Qur'an, 78:14-16)

«For that We pour forth water in abundance,
And We split the earth in fragments,
And produce therein corn,
And grapes and nutritious plants,
And olives and dates,
And enclosed gardens, dense with lofty trees,
And fruits and fodder —
For use and convenience to you and your cattle».

(Qur'an, 80: 25-32)

«O you people! Worship your Sustainer.... Who has made the earth your couch and the heavens your canopy; and sent down rain from the heavens; and brought forth therewith fruits for your sustenance; then set not up rivals unto God when you know [the truth]».

(Qur'an, 2: 21-2)

«Or who has made the earth firm to live in; made rivers in its midst; set thereon mountains immovable, and made a separating bar between the bodies of flowing water? [Can there be another] god besides God? Nay, most of them know not».

(Qur'an, 27: 61)

The earth is also important in regard to the concept of mutual relations.

Human beings are created from two of its elements: earth and water. Thus, if man becomes alienated from the earth, he becomes alienated from his very nature. He is not the lord and ruler of the earth; he is a humble member of it.

The superior qualities and faculties he possesses require not that he irresponsibly consumes and destroys its beauties and resources, but that he acts in awareness of his great responsibility towards them.

«And God has produced you from the earth, growing [gradually],
And in the end He will return you into the [earth], and raise you forth [again at the resurrection]?
And God has made the earth for you a carpet [spread out],
That you may go about therein, in spacious roads».

(Qur'an, 71: 17-20)

The word "earth" (ard) is mentioned twice in these short verses. A clear indication of its importance is the fact that it is mentioned 485 times in the Qur'an as a whole and is portrayed as being offered for man's convenience:

«It is He Who has made the earth manageable for you, so traverse through its tracts and enjoy of the sustenance which He furnishes».

(Qur'an, 67: 15).

«It is He Who has made the earth manageable for you, so traverse through its tracts and enjoy of the sustenance which He furnishes».

(Qur'an, 67:15)

«[They will be] among Lote-trees without thorns,
Among Talh trees with flowers [or fruits] piled one above another —

In shade long-extended,
By water flowing constantly,
And fruit in abundance,
Whose season is not limited, nor [supply] forbidden».

(Qur'an, 56:28-33).

These verses and those similar to them have been sources of inspiration for Muslims and they have looked on nature in their light.

They have regarded the universe and nature from this Qur'anic point of view.

One can see the finest examples of this in the works of Muslim thinkers, and particularly the great Sufi masters.

We shall suffice here with only two examples.

The first is Mawlana Jalaluddin Rumi, a thinker of the 13th century:

«How does this lifeless cloud know when it has to pour down rain? And you see the earth, which holds this flower and produces ten in its place. Someone is doing these things. It is He that you have to see».

«Despite being lifeless, even the earth knows everything God has bestowed on it. How could it otherwise have accepted the rain, suckled all the plants and nurtured them?».

«The world is being re-created and renewed at every breath, but we are unaware of this, for we see it as static».

Our second example is from Bediuzzaman Said Nursi, a contemporary scholar from Turkey.
The same verses are reflected as follows in his heart:

«Glory be to the One who made the garden of the earth an exhibition of His art, a gathering of His creatures, a place of manifestation of His power, the means of His wisdom, the flower-bed of His mercy, the tillage of Paradise, a place of passage of creatures, for the flood of beings, a funnel for His artefacts.
The adorned animals, decorative birds, fruit-bearing trees, and flowering plants are miracles of His knowledge, wonders of His art, gifts of His munificence, propitious signs of His grace.
The blossoms smiling at the embellished fruits, the birds twittering in the breezes of the early morn, the pattering of the rain on the petals of the flowers, the tender affection of mothers for their infants and young all show to jinn and men, and spirits and living creatures, and angels and spirit beings a Loving One making Himself known, a Merciful One making Himself loved, a Tenderly Kind One bestowing His mercy, a Gracious Bestower manifesting His kindness».

The earth is also considered by Islam to be a place of purification and worship of God.
God's Messenger (PBUH) said:

«The earth was made a place of worship and purification for me [and Muslims]».

And:

«The meaning of this is that when water is not available before worship, earth may used for canonical ablutions (tayammum) in its place». [Bukhari, i, 86]

God's Messenger (PBUH) was emphasizing this point when he said: «God is beautiful and He loves the beautiful; He is generous and loves generosity; He is clean and loves cleanliness».

One should not therefore be surprised at the Islamic view related to the environment, that "everyone should remind each other to conserve and protect the earth." They should not hang back diffidently while the earth is being spoiled. They should attach the greatest importance to cleanliness and purity, physical and particularly moral and spiritual.

3. The Importance of Cleanliness

Islam considers cleanliness to be one of the fundamentals of belief. It thus makes a direct connection between belief and cleanliness.

It is because of this that throughout the ages cleanliness has been one of the Muslims' most striking characteristics.

In one Hadith, God's Messenger (PBUH) says: "Cleanliness is half of belief." [Muslim, Tahara, 1.]

Some of the earliest verses revealed to him by God were:

O you wrapped up [in a mantle]! Arise and deliver your warning! And your Sustainer magnify! And your garments keep free from stain! And all abomination shun!

(Qur'an, 74:1-5)

It may be noted here that by requiring the cleanliness of clothes, on the one hand physical cleanliness is being emphasized, and by demanding that "abomination" is shunned, on the other moral and spiritual purity are being underlined.

Thus, in Islam, physical and moral and spiritual cleanliness form an indivisible whole.

Muslims should neglect neither the cleanliness of their surroundings, houses, the roads they use, and parks and gardens, nor any sort of moral and spiritual cleanliness.

The clearest example of this approach in Islamic life may be seen in the Six Books of Prophetic Hadiths, the chief and most reliable source of Islamic civilization.

On looking at these books, it is seen that the sections on cleanliness come at the beginning.

This shows clearly the priority the religion and civilization give to cleanliness.

The Qur'an says:

> O you who believe! When you prepare for prayer, wash your faces, and your hands [and arms] to the elbows; rub your heads [with water]; and [wash] your feet to the ankles. If you are in a state of ceremonial impurity, bathe your whole body...
>
> (Qur'an, 5:6).

As is seen, the first condition of the obligatory prayers — which are the foundation of Islam, the support of religion, and 'Ascension' of the believers — is cleanliness.

The Qur'an therefore commands that at least five times a day we wash those parts of the body that may become dirtied like the hands, face, nose, ears, mouth, neck, head, and feet, and that we keep them clean.

The place the prayers are to be performed also has to be clean, as well as the clothes worn.

Another dimension of the Islamic approach to cleanliness is apparent in the Divine Name of Most Holy (Qudduûs), one of *God's Most Beautiful Names* (al-Asma al-Husna).

In his explanations of this Divine Name, Bediuzzaman Said Nursi points out the cleanness of the universe, and states that the face of the earth and such beings as the clouds, rain, flies, crows, maggots, earthworms, ants, various insects, and the red and white corpuscles in the human body all manifest the Name of Most Holy in their functions, and carry out duties as "cleansing officials."

Throughout his life the Prophet Muhammad (PBUH) paid the greatest attention to cleanliness of every sort.

For instance, he was always careful when going to the mosque or to visit someone or when being in the company of others to wear clean and presentable clothes, to rub fragrant scents on himself, and not to eat things like onion and garlic which would be unpleasant to others.

It is clear then that Muslims are obliged to always be clean in every respect, both physical and moral and spiritual.

A Muslim who pays attention to physical cleanliness, that is, who keeps his body, house, and surroundings clean, will not neglect the purity of his heart and spirit and his moral purity — it is not possible that he neglects these.

We all know that the most important condition for protecting ourselves against illness is being clean and living in a clean environment.

What preventative medicine tells us is nothing different to this. Also, we should never forget this admonition of the Qur'an:

«God loves those who turn to Him constantly and He loves those who keep themselves pure and clean».

(Qur'an, 2: 222).

4. The Cleanliness of the Social Environment

One of the most important topics that come to mind when one says "environmental health" is the cleanliness of the common environment.

These are places such as roads, places of worship, schools, parks, children's playgrounds, stadiums, excursion spots and picnic places, public lavatories, public beaches, and other such places.

What has to be done to maintain the cleanliness of the social environment is to think not of ourselves but of others.

We should not forget that God's Messenger (PBUH) forbade the dirtying of the roads and paths people used, and the places they sat and rested, like shady places and under trees and walls.

He said that to remove a branch or a thorn that would cause hurt to people as they passed was a part of belief.

He said too that God does not love those who cause hurt and pain to believers.

Muslims should scrupulously avoid doing anything to upset or disturb others in any circumstances or in any place.

To pollute or dirty the city in which one lives, or the town or village and their surrounding countryside, waters, air, or views, and to scatter rubbish and refuse is both a sin and extremely discourteous. It is lack of thought both for oneself and for others. For thoughtful people know that others will be disturbed by any place they have dirtied, and the beauties of nature spoilt.

They are aware that it is an attribute of the believer and a sign of maturity not to leave scattered nutshells, bottles, cans, wrappers, and bits of paper and other refuse in the streets and picnic areas or to do anything that will disturb other people, or even the animals.

5. The Preservation of Trees, Woodland, and Green Areas

5.1. Trees in the Qur'an

The Qur'an by giving meaning to the world we live in and our journey in this life is the fountain and the reference point for Muslims in history and today.

In this sense, the Qur'an has been a source of inspiration, illumination, and guidance for Muslim philosophers, theologians, Sufi masters, scientists, jurists, and average Muslims who have accepted it as their sacred revelation from the first revelation to present day.

We Muslims naturally believe that the Qur'an can and should continue to play such a role today in our quest for conducting a meaningfully ethical life and solving our daunting problems. We have to open our hearts and minds to the Quran so that the light of the Quran would penetrate into our minds and hearts; then enlighten and guide us.

This is a change within yourselves and translate the Quranic values and the exemplary ethics of the Prophet Muhammed (PBUH) with our actions and way of life.

Doubtless, one of the most important aspects of protecting the environment and ecology is the conservation of the trees, forests, woodland, countryside, and all the living creatures whose habitats are such areas.

We see that the religion of Islam puts forward important principles for these too. These noteworthy principles related to the conservation of such areas may be classed as moral and legal.

If we look at the Qur'an, we see that the word "tree" is mentioned with various meanings.

Despite containing no direct command to plant trees, it speaks of trees and gardens and orchards so frequently and descriptively that it is not possible for any attentive reader of the Qur'an not to grow in awareness of them. For when creating this world, God adorned it with trees and gardens and offered them for man's use.

The word "tree" is mentioned 26 times in the Qur'an, and the word "paradise" in the sense of garden around 146 times.

«It is He Who sends down rain from the skies; with it We produce green [crops], out of which we produce grain, heaped up [at harvest]; out of the date-palm and its sheaths [or spathes] [come] clusters of dates hanging low and near; and [then there are] gardens of grapes, and olives, and pomegranates, each similar [in kind] yet different [in variety]; when they begin to bear fruit, feast your eyes with the fruit and the ripeness thereof. Behold! in these things there are signs for people who believe».

(Qur'an, 6: 99)

«It is He Who produces gardens, with trellises and without, and dates, and tilth with produce of all kinds, and olives and pomegranates, similar [in kind] and different [in variety]; eat of their fruit in their season, but render the dues that are proper on the day that the harvest is gathered. But waste not by excess; for God loves not the wasters».

(Qur'an, 6: 141)

«It is He Who sends down rain from the sky. From it you drink, and out of it [grows] the vegetation on which you feed cattle. * With it He produces for you corn, olives, date-palms, grapes, and every kind of fruit. Verily in this is a sign for those who give thought».

(Qur'an, 16: 11)

These verses thus mention the rain, trees, earth, gardens, vineyards and date groves, and clouds; they point out the Divine balance between all the elements making up nature, and want us to take lessons from them.

To put it another way, we are being required to raise our heads in our personal and daily lives and to look at the world about us in a different way. For through their order and systems and ecological balances, all creatures point to their Creator.

In another place, the Qur'an draws our attention to the balance of nature, then indicates that we should be careful to observe the balances and rights in the life of society. That is to say, rights and balances are universal rules that we have to observe:

«The sun and the moon follow courses [exactly] computed;
And the herbs and the trees — both [alike] bow in adoration.
And the firmament He has raised high, and He has set up the balance [of justice], In order that you may not transgress [due] balance.
So, establish weight with justice and fall not short in the balance!».
(Qur'an, 55: 5-9)

It is clear that the Islamic worldview could not endorse any view of man's vicegerency of the earth which destroys and spoils the ecological balances and the order and systems of nature, which it teaches that God has created and put as signs of His own existence.

For vicegerent (khalifa) means 'deputy'. And this in turn means that man is the sole being whom God holds responsible for the earth, to whom He has entrusted its preservation. Such a deputy would not betray the trust of the One who created the world with a particular order, balance, and harmony. If he was to spoil the order and harmony and destroy them, he would be known as an unreliable and perfidious deputy.

5.2. Trees and Woodlands in Hadiths of the Prophet (PBUH)

Both in his practices and in various of his Hadiths, the Prophet Muhammad (PBUH) attached great importance to planting trees, protecting existent ones, planting forests, as well as to conserving existent ones. A'isha, one of his wives, said: "His character was the Qur'an." [Muslim, Musafirun, 139] His practices and conduct related to conservation of the environment should therefore be considered from the Qur'anic standpoint. For us his actions are sources of inspiration constituting his Sunna or practices, which we are obliged to follow.

To put it another way, as in all matters, the exemplar of Islamic conduct related to the environment and the person who displayed it in most perfect fashion was God's Messenger (PBUH). As this, and his commands concerning it, are learnt, our weighty responsibilities become clear. Some Hadiths of the Prophet connected with planting trees and protecting them:

«If you have a sapling, if you have the time, be certain to plant it, even if Doomsday starts to break forth».

[al-Munawi, Fayd al-Qadir, iii, 30.]

«Whoever plants trees, God will give him reward to the extent of their fruit».

[Musnad, v, 415.]

«Whoever reclaims and cultivates dry, barren land will be rewarded by God for the act. So long as men and animals benefit from it He will record it for him as almsgiving».

[al-Munawi, Fayd al-Qadir, vi, 39]

«Whoever plants a tree, reward will be recorded for him so long as it produces fruit».

[Majma' al-Zawaid, v, 480.]

«If a Muslim plants a tree, that part of its produce consumed by men will be as almsgiving for him. Any fruit stolen from the tree will also be as almsgiving for him. That which the birds eat will also be as almsgiving for him. Any of its produce which people may eat thus diminishing it, will be as almsgiving for the Muslims who planted it».

[Muslim, Musaqat, 2 No: 2.]

«The reward accruing from seven things continue to reach the person concerned even if he is in his grave: knowledge he has taught, water he has provided for the public benefit, any well he has dug, any tree he has planted, a mosque he has built, recitations of the Qur'an bequeathed to him, and children who pray for him after his death».

[al-Munawi, Fayd al-Qadir, iv, 87.]

On migrating to Medina, God's Messenger (PBUH) organized the planting of trees and of date groves.

He made the forests and green spaces conservation areas, where every sort of living creature lived.

These were called sanctuaries (hima). For example, a strip of land approximately twelve miles wide around Medina was proclaimed a sanctuary and made a conservation area.

We know that he proclaimed other areas, similar to this, sanctuaries.

All these show the paramount importance — as a religion — Islam gives to nature conservancy and protection of all nature's living creatures.

Following these commands of the Qur'an and the exemplary practices of God's Messenger (PBUH), throughout history Muslims have given importance to planting trees and protecting existing one's.

Abu Bakr, the first Caliph, for example, when sending an expedition for a battle to Muta, gave some instructions and underlines that: "Do not cut down trees and do not kill animals except food (in the enemy territory)".

Green is the colour of Islamic civilization, so too the dome of Prophet's tomb is green. These are not mere coincidence; they should be seen as reflecting the importance Islam gives to greenery, nature, and trees.

6. The Protection of Animals

Another important question related to the environment is the good treatment of the animals in our lives, and the protection of them; or more correctly, extending our kindness and compassion to them. However, today many animal species are becoming extinct. Other animals stray abandoned and hungry in the streets.

Taken as a whole, therefore, it cannot be said that we treat animals well and carry out our duties towards them.

In my view, one of the most important reasons for this is our indifference towards Islamic values. For Islam regulates not only relations between individuals and between individuals and society and the state, it also regulates relations between man and nature and man and the environment.

A natural consequence of this is that man is answerable to God for his attitude and actions towards nature and animals. This may be seen in the following Hadith of the Prophet (PBUH):

«If without good reason anyone kills a sparrow, or a creature lesser than that even, the living creature will put his plaint to God on the Day of Judgement, saying: 'So-and-so killed me for no purpose».

[Nasai, Sayd, 34.]

Thus, it is stressed that the purposeless and arbitrary killing of the living creatures of nature, whether large or small, is prohibited, and that those who do so will be called to account by God on the Last Day.

6.1. Animals in the Qur'an

On looking at the Qur'an, the prominent place given animals, the key members of the eco system, is immediately apparent. A number of its Suras bear animals' names: al-Baqara (The Cow); al-Nahl (The Bee), al-Anqabut (The Spider), al-Naml (The Ant).

One of the striking expressions the Qur'an uses about animals is that they are a "community" (umma). It is especially noteworthy that this concept, which is a significant concept in Islamic tradition and literature, should also be used for animals:

«There is not an animal [that lives] on the earth, nor a being that flies on its wings, but [forms part of] communities like you. Nothing have We omitted from the Book, and they [all] shall be gathered to their Lord in the end».

(Qur'an, 6:38)

The Qur'an also portrays animals as works of art displaying the Maker's skill and perfection:

«And verily in cattle [too] will you find an instructive sign. For what is within their bodies, between excretions and blood, we produce, for your drink, milk, pure and agreeable to those who drink it».

(Qur'an, 16:66)

«Do they not look at the Camels how they are made? And at the Sky how it is raised high? And at the Mountains How they are fixed firm? And at the Earth how it is spread out?».

(Qur'an, 88:17-20)

These verses invite man to contemplate four things, which they can see in every-day life, and which are full of meaning, high design, and the goodness of God to man. As we know camel is a domesticated animal, which for Arab countries is par excellence the Camel. What a wonderful structure pas this Ship of the Desert? He can store water in his stomach for days. He can live on dry and thorny desert shrubs. His limb are adapted to his life. And withal, he is so gentle! Who can sign his praises enough?

6.2. Animals in Hadiths of the Prophet (PBUH)

As with the important place given to animals by the Qur'an, the Prophet Muhammad (PBUH) also insisted on the protection of animals and the kind treatment of them. His concern that they should be well treated, protected, and not abused or degraded is truly noteworthy. While at the present time torture and oppression of every sort are meted out to man, whom God created as the noblest of creatures, the Prophet prohibited torture and abuse of animals even.

Thus, God's Messenger (PBUH) taught that Muslims should act kindly not only towards human beings but to all living beings:

«The Most Merciful One is merciful towards those who are merciful. Act kindly to those on the earth so that those in the heavens [the angels] will be merciful to you». [Tirmidhi, Birr, 16.]

And as given above: "Anyone who kills a sparrow without good reason will be called to account by God at the Last Judgement." God's Messenger (PBUH) also commanded that birds' nests should not be disturbed, or the eggs or chicks stolen. [Bukhari, al-Adab al-Mufrad, 139.]

On one occasion, he ordered someone who had filled his bag with fledglings stolen from nests and brought them to the town to return them to their nests immediately.

The young birds were thus able to grow to maturity in natural surroundings in their mothers' nests.

We learn of another example which reflects clearly the essence of Islamic civilization and how it regards animals from 'Abdullah ibn Mas'ud, one of the Prophet's close Companions:

«We were on a journey with God's Messenger when we came across a bird the size of a sparrow with two chicks. We seized the chicks, whereupon the hen started beating its wings and screeching. God's Messenger turned and when he saw what we had done, asked: 'Who separated those chicks from their mother? Return them at once!' So we left them free».[Abu Dau'd, Jihad, 122, No: 2675; iii, 125-6.]

The Prophet Muhammad (PBUH) thus enjoined the protection of animals and birds, that they should not be ill-treated, but should be well looked after and kept clean, and employed in work suitable to their natures, and should not be loaded with burdens greater than they can bear. He put a ban on hunting, forbidding the arbitrary hunting of animals for pleasure. He one day related the following story to those sitting by him:

«A traveller felt a great thirst as he went on his way, so stopped at well and drank of its water. As he came up from the well he saw a dog licking the damp soil with its thirsty, lolling tongue.
Saying to himself: 'This animal is thirsty like I was,' he went back down to the well and filled his shoe with water. Then holding it firm returned and held it for the dog to drink. God praised that servant of His for his act and forgave all his sins."
His Companions then asked him:
"So are we rewarded for watering animals?"
God's Messenger replied: "There is a reward for giving any living creature to drink"». [Bukhari, Tajrid al-Sahih, vii, 223, No: 1066.]

God's Messenger (PBUH) prohibited the ill-treatment of animals, and warned us concerning this question when he said:

«A woman was sent to Hell because she tied up her cat and neither gave it food nor allowed it free to hunt the cockroaches». [Bukhari, Adhan, 90]

God's Messenger stated that like men, animals employed in various tasks had the right to rest, and when stopping to rest on journeys, in particular insisted that the animals' needs should be met and that they should be rested. Anas ibn Malik, one of the Companions, related:

«Whenever we arrived at a stopping-place, we would never start the prayers until we had removed the loads from the pack-animals [and left them free to rest]». [Abu Dau'd, Jihaad, 48.]

Reynold A. Nicholson, for example, is very impressed by Muslims treatment of animals. In his book *The Mystic of Islam* we find the following story:

«Bayazid [ninetieth century Muslim mystic] purchased some cardamom seed at Hamadhan, and before departing put into his gabardine a small quantity which was left over. On reaching Bistam and recollecting what he had done, he took out the seed and found out that it contained a number of ants. Saying, "I have carried the poor creatures away from their home" he immediately set off and journeyed back to Hamadhan-a distance of several hundred [724] miles».

We see then that the religion of Islam permits that no living creature is tormented or abused. Whether man or beast, all living creatures have rights. Those who violate their rights or disregard them will be punished in the hereafter by God if it not possible for them to be punished by the authorities here.

God's Messenger (PBUH) expressed this in the following way:

«It is a fact that in the next life you will render their rights to those to whom they are due. The hornless sheep even will receive its right by way of retaliation from a horned sheep that butted it». [Muslim, Birr, 60.]

This stance of the Prophet, and his admonitions, have had a powerful effect on Muslims down the ages. Being imbued with the Prophet's attitude, Muslims have always looked kindly and tolerantly on people. They have never tortured their enemies even. Members of other religions and faiths have lived in security amongst them. Animals too have received their share of this loving, compassionate, and tolerant civilization.

'Izz ad-Din ibn 'Abdas-Salam, the thirteenth century Muslim legal scholar, formulated the following principles of animal rights which appears to be based on the very teaching of the Qur'an and the Sunna of the Prophet (PBUH):

«that he spend on them the provision that their kinds require, even if they have aged or sickened such that no benefit comes from them;

that he not burden them beyond what they can bear;

that he not put them together with anything by which they would be injured, whether of their own kind or other species, whether by breaking their bones or butting or wounding;

that he slaughter them with kindness;

that when he slaughters them he neither flay their skins nor break their bones until their bodies have become cold and their lives he passed away;

that he not slaughter their young within their sight but that he isolate them;

that he make comfortable their resting places and watering places;

that he put their males and females together during their mating seasons;

that he not discard those which he takes as game; and neither shoot them with anything that breaks their bones nor bring about their destruction by any means that renders their meat unlawful to eat».

We saw, moreover, from the Prophet's Hadiths that treating animals well is a means of a person entering Paradise, while ill-treatment of them may be the cause of a person going to Hell.

7. Examples from Islamic History

If one studies the histories of the Muslim peoples, one sees that they lived in harmony with nature and its creatures. The most reliable witnesses to this were Western travelers who visited the Muslim lands. The famous French writer Montaigne touched on this subject when he said: "The Muslim Turks found hospitals and pious foundations for animals even."

The French lawyer Guer, who travelled in the Ottoman Empire in the 17th century, mentioned a hospital in Damascus where sick cats and dogs were treated. While Prof. M. Sibai gives the following details about the pious foundations for animals:

«In the old tradition of pious foundations, areas were allotted for the grazing and treatment of sick animals. The 'Green Mar'a' (the area now covered by Damascus sports stadium) was a place that at one time had been made over to the grazing of helpless animals, which were no longer fed by their owners since they had lost the power to work. Such animals grazed here till their deaths.

Among the pious foundations of Damascus there were also places where cats could eat and sleep and wander about. There were hundreds of cats here which, having no difficulties in finding their daily provender, were like the permanents fixtures of the place.

Birds have always had a special place in Muslims' lives.

They have felt particular affection not only for songbirds like nightingale, but for others such as chiefly the pigeon, and storks, doves, and swallows.

This affection has been manifested in various ways:

the defence of birds' rights, establishing pious foundations for the feeding of birds,

founding hospitals to tend to sick birds,

the taming of some species and keeping them in cages, as well as the opposite of this, setting them free from captivity.

Just as many people have released them from their cages out of love for them, so many others have kept them in cages».

Birds have always had a special place in Muslims' lives. They have felt particular affection not only for songbirds like nightingale, but for others such as chiefly the pigeon, and storks, doves, and swallows. This affection has been manifested in various ways: the defence of birds' rights, establishing pious foundations for the feeding of birds, founding hospitals to tend to sick birds, the taming of some species and keeping them in cages, as well as the opposite of this, setting them free from captivity. Just as many people have released them from their cages out of love for them, so many others have kept them in cages. The famous French poet Lamartine recorded the following observations:

«Muslims have good relations with all creatures, animate and inanimate: trees, birds, dogs, in short, they respect all the things God has created.
They extend their compassion and kindness to all the species of wretched animals which in our countries are abandoned or ill-treated. In all the streets at specific intervals they leave bowls of water for the dogs of the district.
Some Muslims found pious foundations at their deaths for the pigeons they have fed throughout their lives, thus ensuring that grain will be scattered for [the birds] after they have departed».
(Lamartine, 1857).

Edward William Lane (1801–1876), a British Orientalist, translator and lexicographer visited Cairo in 1825. He is well remembered as one of the greatest of nineteenth-century orientalists. His reputation is firmly established with such works as *Manners and Customs of the Modern Egyptians*, his annotated translation of the *Arabian Nights*, and his magisterial *Arabic-English Lexicon*.

As the late Professor Edward Said commented, Lane was "an authority whose use was an imperative for anyone writing or thinking about the Orient, not just about Egypt". Lane adopted the dress of an upper-class Ottoman during his stay in Cairo from 1825 to 1828, and from 1833 to 1835. He explains the reason why he dressed like a Muslim as follows:

«If dressed in the European style, he [the traveler] is seldom molested or insulted: but if habited as a Turk, he commands respect».

«As I approached the shore, I felt like an Eastern bridegroom, about to lift up the veil of his bride, and to see, for the first time, the features which were to charm, or disappoint, or disgust him."
I was not visiting Egypt merely as a traveller, to examine its pyramids and temples and grottoes, and, after satisfying my curiosity, to quit it for other scenes and other pleasures:
I was about to throw myself entirely among strangers; to adopt their language, their customs and their dress; and, in associating almost exclusively with the natives, to prosecute the study of their literature. My feelings therefore, on that occasion, partook too much of anxiety to be very pleasing.
Benevolence and charity to the poor are virtues which the Egyptians possess in an eminent degree, and which are instilled into their hearts by religion; they are as much excited to the giving of alms by the expectation of enjoying corresponding rewards in heaven, as by pity for the distresses of their fellow-creatures, or a disinterested wish to dothe will of God.
The many handsome "Sebeels" or public fountains (buildings erected andendowed for the gratuitous supply of water to passengers), which are seen in this city, and the more humble structures of the same kind in the villages and fields, are monuments of the same virtue». (Lane 2014)

Lane also proved us very vivid impressions how Muslims

treat their animal:

«I was much pleased at observing their humanity to dumb animals; to see a person, who gathered the folds of his loose clothes to prevent their coming in contact with a dog, throw, to the impure animal, a portion of the bread, which he was eating». (ibid)

When Lane visited Cairo ten years later, he surprised the pace of change at Muslims attitudes towards animals:

«I find the generality of theEgyptians very much changed for the worse, with respect to their humanity to brutes and to their fellow-creatures".
"I inclined to think that the conduct of Europeans has greatly conduced to produce this effect, for I do not remember to have seen acts of cruelty to dumb animals except in places where Franks [that is, Europeans 1 either reside or are frequent visitors ...». (ibid)

As history as well as Western travellers of Muslim lands observe, Islam attaches the greatest importance to the conservation of the environment as a whole. For the environment and all the living beings within it are created by God. As human beings, we have been entrusted with conserving and developing it.

The conservation of the environment is therefore not only a human obligation but also a religious obligation. Indeed, believers should undertake this responsibility more than anyone. It is understandable if someone who does not believe in God and the Last Judgement is unconcerned with it, but for a believer to be unconcerned is both incomprehensible and unforgivable. How profound are Yunus Emre's, the Turkish poet of 13th century, words: *"We love creatures for the sake of their Creator"*!

No concerned and believing Muslim individual will forget that he is answerable for how he treats not only men but also all creatures, or that one day he will be called to account for how he acted. With the following verse, the Qur'an warns all Muslims:

«Whoever does an atom's weight of good shall see it,
And whoever does an atom's weight of evil, shall see it».
(Qur'an, 99: 7-8)

8. Not Wasting the Earth's Resources

A further important Islamic principle related to the environment is the Islamic prohibition concerning thoughtless consumption; that is, wastefulness and extravagance.

Wastefulness is not only the thoughtless consumption of natural resources, it is at the same time disrespectful towards God, the Creator and Owner of all the bounties.

For this reason, in Islam, eating and drinking of licit food is lawful, but wastefulness is forbidden. At this time, we know better than at any other that the world's resources are limited. Extravagance and over-consumption will affect not only ourselves, but forthcoming generations. We are therefore compelled to be aware and sensitive concerning this matter.

In the Holy Qur'an, God says:

«Verily We have created all things in proportion and measure».
(Qur'an, 54: 49)

If we keep this in mind, we see that carefully preserving the balance and measure is a human obligation.

The science of ecology shows us that the universe contains extremely sensitive eco systems and balances, and that man has therefore to maintain these ecological systems.

Modern man only came to realize the environmental problems with the help of ecology when the problems became apparent, whereas the Qur'an draws our attention to this balance in particular, which now everyone is trying to maintain.

The obligation of maintaining this balance, which is God's work, is human's, whom God created on *"the best of patterns,"* and who is His vicegerent or deputy on earth.

No Muslim therefore will spoil the universe's balance, nor will any Muslim look on indifferently while other's spoil it.

For the natural balance is at the same time a mirror reflecting Almighty God's Most Beautiful Names.

Islam permits utilization of the environment, but this should not be arbitrary.

Wastefulness and extravagance are prohibited by God:

«O children of Adam! Wear your beautiful apparel at every time and place of prayer; eat and drink, but waste not by excess, for God loves not the wasters».

(Qur'an, 7:31)

The eating and drinking in this verse refer to utilizing the resources necessary for the continuation of our lives. This should not be uncontrolled.

The elements that support life should be conserved so that they can be utilized continuously. More than this, such conservation should be unselfish. That is, it should not only have human interests in view.

Thus, while utilizing the world's bounties, the Muslim should not do so with an unconstrained and irresponsible approach to consumption. On the contrary, he is obliged to base all such actions and the measure of his consumption on Islamic economic principles.

Every passing day it is becoming better understood that the world's resources are limited. The following commands of the Qur'an are striking at a time feasible development and economic models are being widely discussed:

«And render to the kindred their due rights, as [also] to those in want, and to the wayfarer; but squander not [your wealth] in the manner of a spendthrift.
Verily spendthrifts are brothers of the Evil Ones and the Evil One is to his Lord [Himself] ungrateful». (Qur'an, 17:26-7)

«Those who, when they spend, are not extravagant and not niggardly, but hold a just [balance] between those extremes».

(Qur'an, 25:67)

The Qur'an commands us to eat and drink, but waste not by excess, for God loves not the wasters so that we become accustomed to avoiding wastefulness and extravagance in our daily consumption of food and drink.

It frequently points out that frugality and consuming what one has without being over-lavish is the measure of what God loves.

In some verses, Almighty God states that He "created every animal from water," showing in a most interesting and meaningful way that water is the basis of life and living.

God's Messenger (PBUH) also attached great importance to water and forbade the excessive use of it even when taking the ablutions, saying that to do so was 'detestable' (makruh).

He thus prevented people using too much water even for something like ablutions, when they are preparing to enter the Divine presence and court.

A Hadith about this is the following:

«God's Messenger (PBUH) appeared while Sa'd was taking the ablutions. When he saw that Sa'd was using a lot of water, he intervened saying:
'What is this? You are wasting water."
Sa'd replied asking: "Can there be wastefulness while taking the ablutions?" To which God's Messenger replied:
"Yes, even if you take them on the bank of a rushing river"».
[Musnad, ii, 22]

While interpreting this Hadith, scholars have pointed out that it does not refer only to using less water while taking the ablutions, but to a basic principle of Islam.

They have emphasized the following points in connection with it:

- God's Messenger is stating an important prohibition.
- The prohibition concerns something for which no effort was exerted in obtaining it, nor money spent, but is free: the water of a flowing river.
- Moreover, the excessive use of water causes no deficiency to nature, nor does it cause pollution, nor spoil the ecological balance.
- It causes no harm to living beings.

Furthermore, the matter in question, that is, taking the ablutions, is not some trivial matter; it is a necessary condition for the obligatory prayers. If then, despite all the above, it is 'detestable' to use excessive water from a river while taking the ablutions and it was prohibited by the Prophet, how much stronger is the proscription on being wasteful and extravagant in some matter in which the above statements are not applicable?

That is, if wastefulness:

- is in something that required the expending of effort, expense, or at least time;
- if it caused deficiency to or pollution of nature, thus spoiling the ecological balance;
- if it harmed living beings;
- if it violated the rights of forthcoming generations to live in a healthy environment;
- if it was arbitrary and meaningless, and merely for enjoyment;
- if it was contrary to the basic aim; then what would the situation be?

The Qur'an and Sunna stipulating that water is the basis of life lays a number of obligations and responsibilities on Muslims: the conserving of existent water supplies in the best possible way; the prevention of any activity that might lead to the pollution of water sources or spoil the purity and characteristics of the water; never adopting an extravagant and irresponsible attitude in the consumption of water; rational and regular utilization of water and water sources.

There are very good reasons for Islam prohibiting wastefulness and prodigality so forcefully. We may put it this way: there are between five and six thousand million people living in the world today. Just think of each individual person cutting down a tree or killing an animal just for the fun of it. Six thousand million trees or six thousand million animals would perish. Or think of the water they would waste, or the bread or other foodstuffs they would throw away.

The serious consequences of those apparently insignificant actions are clear!

Moreover, for the greater part it is not possible to reclaim the resources we have polluted, destroyed, or annihilated. It is in this light that we may understand how meaningful the point God's Messenger (PBUH) was emphasizing when he said: *"Even if you take the ablutions in a flowing river, do not waste the water"* and how important it is for the preservation of the ecological balance.

The world belongs to all of us!

We are all obliged to conserve and protect. We must co-operate and work together for a better world, a better future, and a better environment. We must love and preserve our environment and all the living creatures within it in the name of our Sustainer, Who created them and entrusted them to us. In this way, the 21st century may be the century of peace, happiness, tolerance, and brotherhood. Not only for men, but for all creatures, animate and inanimate.

God created the universe and adorns the skies with the sun, the moon and the stars, and the face of the earth with flowers, trees, gardens, orchards, and the various animal species, oceans, seas, and coral reefs with millions of creatures living there. God causes the rivers and streams to flow, upholds the skies (without support), causes the rain to fall and places the boundary between night and day. Therefore, the universe, with all its richness and vitality, is the work and art of God who creates and sustains all plants and animals as pairs, in this way causing their procreation.

The Qur'an presents a vivid and rich portrayal of the environment, full of meaning, purpose, order and sacred beauty. Nature is seen as a balanced, just, peaceful, unified pattern, created by and functioning according to God's design, each part having its purpose, its role within the interlocking whole. It is thus sacred and valuable in of itself: it reveals God, being a cosmic Qur'an (and is thus a way to cleanliness, not to be wasted).

Therefore, as everything has been created by measure and has an order and then that everything is interdependent with everything else implies that humans should/must consider this *interconnectedness* when dealing and interacting with the natural environment. We have to live a sustainable lifestyle without jeopardizing the life of future generations and other species.

As God has created this world and entrusted it to human beings alone, they are not the owners and masters of the natural environment, as such. They are only trustees and stewardships on the earth. More importantly, this *stewardships* includes the *maintains* and *utilization of the natural environment in accordance with what God created these things for, and to consider the order and the ecological balance of nature* on the other.

In summary, environmental awareness, caring for the environment and animals, deep concern over climate change and its daunting consequences and all other related problems are our ethical and moral responsibility. Therefore, we have to find solutions in the light of the Qur'an and the life of the Prophet.

However, as al-Kindi, the First Muslim philosopher, reminded us in the 10th century *"we should never be ashamed to approve truth and acquire it no matter what its source might be, even if it might have come from foreign peoples and alien nations far removed from us. To him who seeks the truth, no other object is higher in value"*.

So, we can learn from the experiences of different countries, communities, religions, cultures, and traditions. Any Muslim, who is burning for learning, as the makers of Muslims' intellectual history teaches us, must seek knowledge to solve our problems.

The Qur'anic verse, *"O my Lord, increase my knowledge"* was one of the constant prayers of the Prophet of Islam who also asked God to show him "things as they really are".

This prayer of the Prophet has echoed throughout Muslim history in many forms but perhaps its most eloquent expression is by the tenth/sixteenth century Persian Sufi poet and scholar, Abd al-Rahman Jami (d. 1492) who thus prayed to God:

O God, deliver us from the preoccupation with worldly vanities, and 'show us the nature of things as they really are.'
Remove from our eyes the veil of ignorance, and *'show us things as they really are.'* Show us not non-existence as existent, nor cast the veil of non-existence over the beauty of existence.
Make this phenomenal world the mirror to reflect the manifestation of Thy beauty, not a veil to separate and repel us from Thee.
Cause these unreal phenomena of the Universe to be for us

the source of knowledge and insight, not the causes of ignorance and blindness. Our alienation and severance from Thy beauty all proceed from ourselves.
Deliver us from ourselves, and accord to us intimate knowledge of Thee. (Jami 1914, 2).

I conclude this work with the following prayer, which we Muslims say many times during our five daily prayers:

"Our Lord! Give us the best of this world; as well as the best in the Hereafter". (2: 201)

APPENDIX 1
Islamic Declaration on Global Climate Change
August 15, 2015-ISTANBUL

In the name of Allah, Most Merciful, Most Compassionate

PREAMBLE

1.1 God – Whom we know as Allah – has created the universe in all its diversity, richness and vitality: the stars, the sun and moon, the earth and all its communities of living beings. All these reflect and manifest the boundless glory and mercy of their Creator. All created beings by nature serve and glorify their Maker, all bow to their Lord's will. We human beings are created to serve the Lord of all beings, to work the greatest good we can for all the species, individuals, and generations of God's creatures.

1.2 Our planet has existed for billions of years and climate change in itself is not new. The earth's climate has gone through phases wet and dry, cold and warm, in response to many natural factors. Most of these changes have been gradual, such that the forms and communities of life have adjusted accordingly.
There have been catastrophic climate changes that brought about mass extinctions, but over time, life adjusted even to these impacts, flowering anew in the emergence of balanced ecosystems such as those we treasure today.

Climate change in the past was also instrumental in laying down immense stores of fossil fuels from which we derive benefits today. Ironically, our unwise and short-sighted use of these resources is now resulting in the destruction of the very conditions that have made our life on Earth possible.

1.3 The pace of Global climate change today is of a different order of magnitude from the gradual changes that previously occurred throughout the most recent era, the Cenozoic. Moreover, it is human-induced: we have now become a force dominating nature.
The epoch in which we live has increasingly been described in geological terms as the Anthropocene, or "Age of Humans".
Our species, though selected to be a caretaker or steward (*khalīfah*) on the earth, has been the cause of such corruption and devastation on it that we are in danger ending life as we know it on our planet. This current rate of climate change cannot be sustained, and the earth's fine equilibrium (*mīzān*) may soon be lost. As we humans are woven into the fabric of the natural world, its gifts are for us to savour. But the same fossil fuels that helped us achieve most of the prosperity we see today are the main cause of climate change. Excessive pollution from fossil fuels threatens to destroy the gifts bestowed on us by God – gifts such as a functioning climate, healthy air to breathe, regular seasons, and living oceans. But our attitude to these gifts has been short-sighted, and we have abused them.
What will future generations say of us, who leave them a degraded planet as our legacy? How will we face our Lord and Creator?

1.4 We note that the Millennium Ecosystem Assessment (UNEP, 2005), backed by over 1300 scientists from 95 countries, found that "overall, people have made greater changes to ecosystems in the last half of the 20th century than at any time in human history... these changes have enhanced human well-being, but have been accompanied by ever increasing degradation (of our environment)."

> "Human activity is putting such a strain on the natural functions of the earth that the ability of the planet's ecosystems to sustain future generations can no longer be taken for granted."

1.5 Nearly ten years later, and in spite of the numerous conferences that have taken place to try to agree on a successor to the Kyoto Protocol, the overall state of the earth has steadily deteriorated.
A study by the Intergovernmental Panel on Climate Change (IPCC) comprising representatives from over 100 nations, published in March 2014, gave five reasons for concern. In summary, they are:

- Ecosystems and human cultures are already at risk from climate change;
- Risks resulting from climate change caused by extreme events such as heat waves, extreme precipitation and coastal flooding are on the rise;
- These risks are unevenly distributed, and are generally greater for the poor and disadvantaged communities of every country, at all levels of development;
- Foreseeable impacts will affect adversely the earth's biodiversity, the goods and services

provided by our ecosystems, and our overall global economy;
- The earth's core physical systems themselves are at risk of abrupt and irreversible changes.

We are driven to conclude from these warnings that there are serious flaws in the way we have used natural resources – the sources of life on Earth. An urgent and radical reappraisal is called for. Humankind cannot afford the slow progress we have seen in all the COP (Conference of Parties – climate change negotiations) processes since the Millennium Ecosystem Assessment was published in 2005, or the present deadlock.

1.6 In the brief period since the Industrial Revolution, humans have consumed much of the non-renewable resources which have taken 250 million years to produce in the earth – all in the name of economic development and human progress. We note with alarm the combined impacts of rising per capita consumption together with the rising human population. We also note with alarm the multi-national scramble now taking place for more fossil fuel deposits under the dissolving ice caps in the arctic regions. We are accelerating our own destruction through these processes.

1.7 Leading climate scientists now believe that a rise of two degrees centigrade in global temperature, which is considered to be the "tipping point", is now very unlikely to be avoided if we continue with business-as-usual; other leading climate scientists consider 1.5 degrees centigrade to be a more likely "tipping point". This is the point considered to be the threshold for catastrophic climate change, which will expose yet more millions of people and countless other creatures to drought, hunger and flooding. The brunt of this will continue to be borne by the poor, as the earth experiences a drastic increase in levels of carbon in the atmosphere brought on in the period since the onset of the industrial revolution.

1.8 It is alarming that in spite of all the warnings and predictions, the successor to the Kyoto Protocol which should have been in place by 2012, has been delayed. It is essential that all countries, especially the more developed nations, increase their efforts and adopt the proactive approach needed to halt and hopefully eventually reverse the damage being wrought.

WE AFFIRM

2.1 We affirm that Allah is the Lord and Sustainer (*Rabb*) of all beings:

الْحَمْدُ لِلَّـهِ رَبِّ الْعَالَمِينَ

«Praise be to Allah, Lord and Sustainer of all beings» (1: 1)
He is the One Creator – He is *Al-Khāliq*:

هُوَ اللَّهُ الْخَالِقُ الْبَارِئُ الْمُصَوِّرُ

«He is Allah – the Creator, the Maker, the Giver of Form» (59: 24).

الَّذِي أَحْسَنَ كُلَّ شَيْءٍ خَلَقَهُ

«He Who has perfected everything He has created» (32: 7).

Nothing that He creates is without value! Each thing is created *bi 'l-haqq*, in truth and for right.

وَمَا خَلَقْنَا السَّمَاوَاتِ وَالْأَرْضَ وَمَا بَيْنَهُمَا لَاعِبِينَ مَا خَلَقْنَاهُمَا إِلَّا بِالْحَقِّ

«And We did not create the heavens and earth and all that is between them in jest. We have not created them but in truth». (44: 38-39)

2.2 We affirm that He encompasses all of His creation – He is *Al-Muhīt*.

وَلِلَّهِ مَا فِي السَّمَاوَاتِ وَمَا فِي الْأَرْضِ وَكَانَ اللَّهُ بِكُلِّ شَيْءٍ مُحِيطًا

«All that is in the heavens and the earth belongs to Allah. Allah encompasses all things». (4: 126)

2.3 We affirm that –

I. God created the earth in perfect equilibrium *(mīzān)*;
II. By His immense mercy we have been given fertile land, fresh air, clean water and all the good things on Earth that make our lives here viable and delightful;
III. The earth functions in natural seasonal rhythms and cycles: a climate in which living beings – including humans – thrive;
IV. The present climate change catastrophe is a result of the human disruption of this balance –

وَالسَّمَاءَ رَفَعَهَا وَوَضَعَ الْمِيزَانَ

أَلَّا تَطْغَوْا فِي الْمِيزَانِ

$$\text{وَأَقِيمُوا الْوَزْنَ بِالْقِسْطِ وَلَا تُخْسِرُوا الْمِيزَانَ}$$

$$\text{وَالْأَرْضَ وَضَعَهَا لِلْأَنَامِ}$$

«He raised the heaven and established the balance so that you would not transgress the balance. Give just weight – do not skimp in the balance. He laid out the earth for all living creatures». (55: 7-10).

2.4 We affirm the natural state (*fitrah*) of God's creation –

$$\text{فَأَقِمْ وَجْهَكَ لِلدِّينِ حَنِيفًا فِطْرَةَ اللَّهِ الَّتِي فَطَرَ النَّاسَ عَلَيْهَا}$$
$$\text{لَا تَبْدِيلَ لِخَلْقِ اللَّهِ ذَلِكَ الدِّينُ الْقَيِّمُ وَلَكِنَّ أَكْثَرَ النَّاسِ لَا يَعْلَمُونَ}$$

«So set your face firmly to the faith in pure devotion, the natural pattern on which Allah made humankind.
There shall be no changing Allah's creation.
That is the true Way, but most people do not know». (30: 30).

2.5 We recognize the corruption (*fasād*) that humans have caused on Earth in our relentless pursuit of economic growth and consumption. Its consequences have been –

1. Global climate change, which is our present concern, in addition to:
2. Contamination and befoulment of the atmosphere, land, inland water systems, and seas;

3. Soil erosion, deforestation and desertification;
4. Destruction, degradation, and fragmentation of the habitats of the earth's communities of life, with devastation of some of the most biologically diverse and productive ecosystems such as rainforests, freshwater wetlands, and coral reefs;
5. Impairment of ecosystem benefits and services;
6. Introduction of invasive alien species and genetically modified organisms;
7. Damage to human health, including a host of modern-day diseases.

ظَهَرَ الْفَسَادُ فِي الْبَرِّ وَالْبَحْرِ بِمَا كَسَبَتْ أَيْدِي النَّاسِ لِيُذِيقَهُم بَعْضَ الَّذِي عَمِلُوا لَعَلَّهُمْ يَرْجِعُونَ

«Corruption has appeared on land and sea by what people's own hands have wrought, that He may let them taste some consequences of their deeds, so that they may turn back». (30: 41)

2.6 We recognize that we are but a minuscule part of the divine order, yet within that order we are exceptionally powerful beings, and have the responsibility to establish good and avert evil in every way we can.
We also recognize that –

- We are but one of the multitude of living

beings with whom we share the earth;
- We have no right to abuse the creation or impair it;
- Intelligence and conscience should lead us, as our faith commands, to treat all things with care and awe (*taqwā*) of their Creator, compassion (*rahmah*) and utmost good (*ihsān*).

وَمَا مِن دَآبَّةٍ فِي الأَرْضِ وَلاَ طَائِرٍ يَطِيرُ بِجَنَاحَيْهِ إِلاَّ أُمَمٌ أَمْثَالُكُم

«There is no animal on the earth, nor any bird that wings its flight but is a community like you». (6: 38)

لَخَلْقُ السَّمَاوَاتِ وَالأَرْضِ أَكْبَرُ مِنْ خَلْقِ النَّاسِ وَلَكِنَّ أَكْثَرَ النَّاسِ لا يَعْلَمُونَ

«The creation of the heavens and the earth is greater than the creation of humankind, but most people don't know ».(40:57)

2.7 We recognize that we are accountable for all our actions

فَمَن يَعْمَلْ مِثْقَالَ ذَرَّةٍ خَيْرًا يَرَهُ
وَمَن يَعْمَلْ مِثْقَالَ ذَرَّةٍ شَرًّا يَرَهُ

«Then whoever has done an atom's weight of good, shall see

it, and whoever has done an atom's weight of evil, shall see it». (99: 7-8).

2.8 In view of these considerations we affirm that our responsibility as Muslims is to act according to the example of the Prophet Muhammad (God's peace and blessings be upon him), who –

- Declared and protected the rights of all living beings, outlawed the custom of burying infant girls alive, prohibited wanton killing of living beings for sport, guided his companions to conserve water even in washing for prayer, forbade the felling of trees in the desert, ordered a man who had taken some nestlings from their nest to return them to their mother, and when he came upon a man who had lit a fire on an anthill, commanded, "Put it out, put it out!";
- Established inviolable zones (*harams*) around Makkah and Al-Madinah, within which native plants may not be felled or cut and wild animals may not be hunted or disturbed;
- Established protected areas (*himās*) for the conservation and sustainable use of rangelands, plant cover, and wildlife;
- Lived a frugal life, free of excess, waste, and ostentation;

- Renewed and recycled his meagre possessions by repairing or giving them away;
- Ate simple, healthy food, which only occasionally included meat;
- Took delight in the created world; and
- Was, in the words of the Qur'an, "a mercy to all beings."

WE CALL

3.1 We call upon the Conference of the Parties (COP) to the United Nations Framework Convention on Climate Change (UNFCCC) and the Meeting of the Parties (MOP) to the Kyoto Protocol taking place in Paris this December, 2015 to bring their discussions to an equitable and binding conclusion, bearing in mind –

- The scientific consensus on global climate change, which is to stabilize greenhouse gas concentration in the atmosphere at a level that would prevent dangerous anthropogenic interference with the climate systems;
- The need to set clear targets and monitoring systems;
- The dire consequences to the planet Earth if we do not do so;

- The enormous responsibility the COP shoulders on behalf of the rest of humanity, including leading us to a new way of relating to God's Earth.

3.2 We particularly call on the well-off nations and oil-producing states to –

- Lead the way in phasing out their greenhouse gas emissions as early as possible and no later than the middle of the century;
- Provide generous financial and technical support to the less well-off to achieve a phase-out of greenhouse gasses as early as possible;
- Recognize the moral obligation to reduce consumption so that the poor may benefit from what is left of the earth's non-renewable resources;
- Stay within the '2 degree' limit, or, preferably, within the '1.5 degree' limit, bearing in mind that two-thirds of the earth's proven fossil fuel reserves remain in the ground;
- Re-focus their concerns from unethical profit from the environment, to preserving it and e-levating the condition of the world's poor.
- Invest in the creation of a green economy.

3.3 We call on the people of all nations and their leaders to –

- Aim to phase out greenhouse gas emissions as soon as possible in order to stabilize greenhouse gas concentrations in the atmosphere;
- Commit themselves to 100 % renewable energy and/or a zero emissions strategy as early as possible, to mitigate the environmental impact of their activities;
- Invest in decentralized renewable energy, which is the best way to reduce poverty and achieve sustainable development;
- Realize that to chase after unlimited economic growth on a planet that is finite and already overloaded is not viable.
  Growth must be pursued wisely and in moderation; placing a priority on increasing the resilience of all, and especially the most vulnerable, to the climate change impacts already underway and expected to continue for many years to come.
- Set in motion a fresh model of wellbeing, based on an alternative to the current financial model, which depletes resources, degrades the environment, and deepens inequality.
- Prioritise adaptation efforts with appropriate support to the vulnerable countries with the

least capacity to adapt, and to vulnerable groups, including indigenous peoples, women, and children.

3.4 We call upon corporations, finance, and the business sector to –

- Shoulder the consequences of their profit-making activities, and take a visibly more active role in reducing their carbon footprint and other forms
of impact upon the natural environment;
- In order to mitigate the environmental impact of their activities, commit themselves to 100 % renewable energy and/or a zero emissions strategy as early as possible and shift investments into renewable energy;
- Change from the current business model, which is based on an unsustainable escalating economy, and adopt a circular economy that is wholly sustainable;
- Pay more heed to social and ecological responsibilities, particularly to the extent that they extract and utilize scarce resources;
- Assist in the divestment from the fossil fuel driven economy and the scaling up of renewable energy and other ecological alternatives.

3.5 We call on all groups to join us in collaboration, co-operation, and friendly competition in this endeavour, and we welcome the significant contributions taken by other faiths, as we can all be winners in this race –

وَلَكِن لِيَبْلُوَكُمْ فِي مَا آتَاكُم فَاسْتَبِقُوا الْخَيْرَاتِ

«But that He (God) may try you in that which He has given you: So vie with one another in doing good deeds». (5: 48)

If we each offer the best of our respective traditions, we may yet see a way through our difficulties.

3.6 Finally, we call on all Muslims wherever they may be –

>Heads of state
>Political leaders
>Business community
>UNFCCC delegates
>Religious leaders and scholars
>Mosque congregations
>Islamic endowments (*awqāf*)
>Educators and educational institutions
>Community leaders
>Civil society activists
>Non-governmental organisations
>Communicators and media

to tackle habits, mindsets, and the root causes of climate change, environmental degradation, and the loss of biodiversity in their particular spheres of influence, following the example of the Prophet Muhammad (peace and blessings be upon him),and bring about a resolution to the challenges that now face us. Allah says in the Qur'an –

وَلاَ تَمْشِ فِي الأَرْضِ مَرَحًا إِنَّكَ لَن تَخْرِقَ الأَرْضَ وَلَن تَبْلُغَ الْجِبَالَ طُولاً

«Do not strut arrogantly on the earth.
You will never split the earth apart nor will you ever rival the mountains' stature». (17: 37).

We bear in mind the words of our Prophet (peace and blessings be upon him):

«The world is sweet and verdant, and verily Allah has made

you stewards in it, and He sees how you acquit your-selves».
(Hadīth related by Muslim from AbūSa'īd Al-Khudrī)

APPENDIX 2
Judaic, Christian, and Islamic Perspectives on Shared Moral Principles

Authors

Jame Schaefer, *Associate Professor, Department of Theology, Marquette University, Milwaukee, USA;*
IbrahimOzdemir, *Visiting Professor of Philosophy, AboAkademi University, Turku, Finland;*
Jeremy Benstein, *Director of Research & Publications, Heschel Center for Environmental Learning, Tel Aviv, Israel;*
Fazlun Khalid, *Founder, Islamic Foundation for Ecology and Environmental Science, Birmingham, United Kingdom;*
Nawal Ammar, *Dean and Professor, College of Humanities & Social Science, Rowan University, Glassboro, USA.*

Paper commissioned at the Abrahamic Traditions and En-vironmental Change Workshop, Rhodes, Greece, 23-26 June 2019, sponsored by the Abrahamic Programs for Academic Collaboration in the MENA Region. August 2019.

Using eight common principles identified in prior research on the environmental views of the world religions,[5] col-

---

[5]Research supporting these principles can be found in Kusumita F. Pedersen's "Environmental Ethics in InterreligiousPerspective", in *Explorations in Global Ethics: Comparative Religious Ethics and Interreligious Dialogue*, eds. Sumner B. Twissand Bruce Grelle, 253-290 (Boulder: WestviewPress, 1998).

leagues[6] who participated in the Abrahamic Traditions and Environmental Change Workshop in Rhodes, Greece, 23-26 June 2019[7]volunteered to indicate the extent to which their traditions — Judaic, Christian, or Islamic — agree with each principle and to provide a citation to a valued source that supports the principle.

The outcome of this compilation provides succinct theological grounding for motivating members of their respective communities in the Middle East and North Africa (MENA) to address ongoing problems of water availability, biological diversity loss, ecosystem-degradation, and human-induced climate change.

Members of their respective communities are strongly urged to return to the sources of their traditions and to reflect on them for meaningful motivation for their actions, including their efforts to collaborate with one another in addressing shared concerns.

---

[6]Jeremy Benstein, The Heschel Sustainability Center, Tel Aviv, Israel, jeremy@heschel.org.ill;

Fazlun Khalid, Islamic Foundation for Ecology and Environmental Sciences, Birmingham, United Kingdom, fazlun.khalid@ifees.org.uk;

Ibrahim Özdemir, Åbo Akademi University, Department of Philosophy, Turku, Finland, ib60dmr@gmail.com;

Nawal Ammar, Dean, College of Humanities andSciences, Rowan University, Glassboro, NJ USA, ammar@rowan.edu;

Jame Schaefer, Marquette University, Department of Theology, Milwaukee, WI USA, schaeferj@marquette.edu, who also compiled and edited the contributions.

[7]Sponsored by the University of Connecticut's Abrahamic Programs for Academic Collaboration in the MENA Region, Al AkhawaynUniversity, andThe Forum on Religion and Ecology at Yale University, the workshop was held in Rhodes, Greece, 23-26 June 2019;

https://abrahamicprograms.uconn.edu/abrahamic_traditions_and_environmental_change

Principle #1: The natural world has value in itself and does not exist solely to serve human needs.

Reflection on Judaic sources yields strong agreement with this principle.

From a biblical perspective, the Genesis 1 story of creation depicts God as valuing each entity created as "good" (Gen 1: 4, 10, 12, 18, 21, 25), a term that implies the intrinsic, inherent value of each type of creature independent of human needs, and God's valuing the totality of creation as "very good" (Gen 1:31), thereby implying its intrinsic, inherent value.

That goodness is a function of its essence and not its utilitarian exchange value according to some human calculus is supported by Rabbinic reflections that discourage thoughts about the superfluousness of any creature (e.g., flies, fleas, mosquitoes, snakes and scorpions) because they are constituents of God's purposeful creation (Talmud Shabbat 77b and parallels).

Maimonides also encouraged valuing all creatures intrinsically when reasoning from Genesis 1 that God purposefully willed the existence of creatures for their own sakes and not for the sake of humans (*Guide to the Perplexed* 3:13).

Christian theologians highlight in commentaries on Genesis 1 that God's attribution of intrinsic value to each created entity and their cumulative goodness should propel the faithful to also value them in themselves through words and actions.

Dwelling on the text's depiction of God's declaring each type of creature "good," John Chrysostom scoffed at anyone who, "bursting with arrogant folly," would contradict God's valuation and urged his listeners to show gratitude to God for all creatures — whether beneficial or harmful to humans

(*Homilies on Genesis* 10.12).

Augustine of Hippo reflected on the goodness of each creature according to its God-given nature (*Nature of the Good* 3) and profusely extolled the goodness of the earth, mountains, fields, air, animals, and other creatures (*On the Trinity* 8.3.4), all of which manifest God's goodness.

Aquinas identified gradations of goodness in creatures according to God-given natures whereby all inanimate and animate creatures constitute an instrumental "order of conservation" in which plants use soil, animals use plants, and human use animals to internally maintain the func-tioning of the universe (e.g., *Summa contra Gentiles* 3.22).

Within this order, all creatures are essential, all are good according to their natures, and all are vital for the functioning of the universe (*Summa theologiae* 1.65.2) that God sustains in existence.

Pope Francis reflects this theological tradition in *Laudato si', On Care of Our Common Home* (2015) in which he underscores the intrinsic value of all creatures apart from their use for humans (#118), the intrinsic value of ecological systems (#140), and the intrinsic value and dignity of the world (#115).

Important for Christians to remember is the traditional understanding of the sacramental quality of the physical, visible world that it mediates God's presence to us, tells us about God's character, and, in its entirety, best manifests God's goodness.

Islam views the natural world as valuable in its relation to God as a totality (*tawḥīd al-khalq*) in which all creatures are dependent upon God for their existence.

Their purposeful creator provides sustenance for them (*Qur'an* 11:6) in a world governed by the principles of unity, balance, and harmony that penetrate every dimension of personal and social life.

All creatures praise God according to their natures and declare God's glory *(Qur'an* 17:44).

From this Islamic perspective, the world does not exist solely to serve human needs (e.g., *Qur'an* 55:10-12).

Humans are creatures among other creatures and dependents among other dependents who should be able to recognize other creatures — animate and inanimate — as signs of God (*e.g., Qur'an* 41:53, 51:20-21, 10:5-6) that display God's skill and perfection (*Qur'an* 16:66).

Principle #2: There is a significant continuity of existence between human and non-human living beings, even though humans have a distinctive role; this continuity can be felt and experienced.

To a great degree, reflections on Judaic sources agree with this principle. Collectively, humans and other species are *adam* made from *adamah* — the earth. The Torah inculcates in us a sense of our modesty and lowliness of which we should be cognizant because we are made of the same stuff as the ass and mule, the cabbage and pomegranate, and even the lifeless stone (Ibn Kaspi, AdneiKesef on Deuteronomy 22:6).

Christian reflections also agree with this principle from their faith perspective that the world of many living creatures has been made possible by God and would not exist if God had not willed and continued to sustain its existence.

All living creatures are related to one another by their creaturehood, dependent on God for their ongoing existence, and able to function in relation to one another to sustain their shared existence.

They also are reliant on non-living creations (e.g., soil, air, water, sun) that God made possible for their sustenance.

Some Christian writers (e.g., Celtic wanderers, English hermits, and Francis of Assisi) underscored the kinship of all animate creatures based on their living experiences with them. Scientific knowledge about the spewing from the furnaces of stars elements that are essential for organic bodies like ours to form, the emergence of life on Earth from single-celled organisms, and the evolution of species strengthen the Christian sense of the continuity of humans with other living beings. These realizations should prompt awe and gratitude to God for the processes through which life emerged and spur Christians to do what most distinguishes humans among creatures — to make and execute informed decisions about living with one another and other species in ways that are mutually beneficial for Earth's flourishing.

In the Islamic tradition, a continuity exists among diverse creatures wherein humankind is given the dignified position of "trustee on earth" (*khalifa*) (*Qur'an* 2:30) who must show humility when carrying out the responsibilities required of trustees. "The creation of the heavens and the earth is far greater than creation of humankind" (*Qur'an* 40:57).

The humblest of God's creation is given the weightiest responsibilities — the price we pay for the privilege of intelligence that God has bestowed on us.

We are accountable to God on the Day of Judgment for how we exercise our special responsibilities as trustees.

Clearly, we are not owners and masters of the natural environment; we are trustees to whom God has delegated the responsibility of maintaining and utilizing the natural environment in accordance with God's intentions.

The *Qur'an* and the prophetic traditions prescribe a criterion for responsible human trusteeship of Earth by refraining from actions that lead to the corruption of the environment: "Do no mischief on the earth after it hath been set in order" (*Qur'an* 7:56).

The Prophet Muhammad is the perfect role model for all Muslims when striving to fulfill their responsibilities.

Principle #3: Non-human beings are morally significant to God and/or in the cosmic order; they have their own unique relations to God, and their own places in the cosmic order.

As indicated in Psalm 145, God's "tender mercy is over all His creatures".

Jewish traditions support the understanding that creatures who are not human are morally significant to God as God's creations, all have their own unique relation to God who cares for them according to their natures, and all have essential roles to play within God's creation.

Reflections by Christian theologians about God's love for all creatures according to their natures and God's care for non-human living creatures by providing for their needs and capabilities through which to nourish themselves imply that they are morally significant for God and should be morally significant for the faithful.

Also supportive of this principle are exclamations by eminent theologians about the goodness, beauty, and integrity of non-human and inanimate creatures — from tiny insects to large mammals, plains to mountain valleys, trees to forests, and streams to wide rivers.

For example, when giving homilies on Genesis 1, Basil of

Caesarea urged his listeners to pay attention to all creatures, to never cease admiring them, and to give glory to God for them (*On the Hexaemeron* 2 and 5).

The traditional Islamic view maintains that all animate creatures constitute communities willed into and sustained in existence by God and conduct themselves in ways that assure their continuity.

The great whales that plough the oceans, elephants of the tropical forests and the ants and bees are examples of creatures forming complex, efficient, multi-generational communities.

Annual mass migrations like the huge flocks of birds that fly each year from one climate zone to another, the movements of reindeer in the tundra and the wildebeest in the African Savannah are striking examples of animals cooperating among members of their species to survive. All have moral significance for God who cares and loves them.

As God's trustees, Muslims have a special responsibility to God for maintaining and utilizing the natural environment in accordance with God's intentions.

Principle #4: The dependence of human life on the natural world can and should be acknowledged in ritual and other expressions of appreciation and gratitude.

Jewish traditions exemplify a deeply embedded range of rituals and other expressions of gratitude to God for the dependence of human life on the natural world.
EretzYisrael, the Land of Israel, is the distinct homeland that is always present and central to traditional Jewish consciousness as demonstrated in liturgies, observances and commandments (mitzvoth) that are applicable only in the Land (e.g.,

tithes on produce and the entire *shemitah* year — a year of release and renewal).

Judaism also has a universal spiritual language pertaining to the environment that is accessible everywhere as manifested in the Jewish calendar that connects the major Jewish holidays to natural cycles and makes these cycles felt in the life of the Jew.

They mark the harvests and the seasons — Passover (*Pesach*) in spring, the Feast of Weeks or Pentecost (*Shavuot*) in early summer, the Festival of Booths (*Sukkot*) in fall, and, the later instituted, the Festival of Lights (Hanukkah) in winter—all of which provide occasions for Jews to express their gratitude to God for the natural world in which they live.

Though the Easter Vigil has been the one annual ritual over the centuries in which Christians recall their dependence on the natural world and express gratitude to God for this gift, the initiation of the Day of Prayer for the Environment in 1989 by His All-Holiness Ecumenical Patriarch Demetrios began a tradition that his successor Patriarch Bartholomew continued from the inception of his patriarchy in 1991.

His many sermons, homilies, prayers, and trips with other religious leaders, scientists, and reporters to endangered areas were concurrent with statements by popes John Paul II and Benedict XVI on the ecological crisis as a moral responsibility for Christians to address, rituals in various Christian denominations, interfaith prayer services, and participation in the Environmental Sabbath in the late 198s and early 1990s during the first weekend in June.

In 2015, Pope Francis joined the Patriarch in renaming September 1 the *World Day of Prayer for the Care of Creation* and together called Christians and the faithful of all religions and spiritualities to reflect on their traditions and how they can act to care for Earth, our common home. When thinking about expressing appreciation and gratitude to God, let us recall Psalm 148 in which all creatures are depicted as giving praise to God in their own "voices" and Francis of Assisi's reworking the psalm with familial language to yield *The Canticle of Creation*.

We must now ask ourselves: Will we — human creatures — join the chorus praising God for the world or continue to cause and allow the dissonance that persists as manifested by the ecological-social crisis?

Muslims recite at the beginning of each of the five daily prayers, "I have turned my face to Him who originated (*fatara*) the heavens and the Earth" (*Qur'an* 6: 79).

This is followed by the Opening (*Fatiha*) of the first chapter of the *Qur'an*: "In the name of God, Most Gracious, Most Merciful. Praise be to God, the Cherisher and Sustainer of the worlds, the Most Gracious, Most Merciful Master of the Day of Judgment. You we worship. Your aid we seek. Show us the straight way, the way of those on whom You have bestowed Your Grace" (1:2-6).

This *Fatiha* is recited seventeen times a day in the observation of the five daily prayers.

These verses have shaped and formed Muslims' perception of the universe and humanity in the past and the present.

The *Qur'an* portrays young Abraham not only as a man burning to learn, but also as a man of faith, commitment, sincerity, hospitality, and integrity.

In his search for meaning, Abraham finds his God as "the Sustainer of all the worlds" who has created us and guides us. God is "the One who gives me to eat and to drink, and when I fall ill, is the One who restores me to health" (*Qur'an* 26:78-80).

The whole creation belongs to God who deserves praise and

gratitude from the faithful.

Clearly, our well-being depends on the well-being of Earth.

Followers of Islam believe that the entirety of Earth is a place of prayer — a sacred space where one can contemplate God.

Daily activities carried out in this space require exemplary behavior; every act is expected to be like a prayer.

Prayer and the natural world are irrevocably connected, and Muslims anticipate that Earth will one day tell how she was treated by humans:

"When the earth is shaken with a (violent) shaking, and the earth reveals what burdens her, and humans say: What has befallen her? On that day she shall tell her story..." (*Qur'an* 99:1-4)

Principle #5 Moral norms such as justice, compassion and reciprocity apply (in appropriate ways) both to human and to non-human beings whose well-being are inseparably connected.

Judaic sources prescribe justice, compassion, and reciprocity toward humans and non-humans, thereby affirming their inseparable connection: Helping the donkey who is struggling or has fallen under a heavy load (Deuteronomy 22:4) even if the donkey is someone else's property, including one's enemy (Exodus 23:5); refraining from yoking a donkey and an ox together (Deuteronomy 22:10) because the weaker will suffer (25:4); and allowing one's animals to rest on Shabbat (Deuteronomy 5:14) that is similar to a labor law aimed at protecting the conditions of the workers.

That animals and humans are part of the same moral community was clear to Jews in antiquity as indicated in

Nineveh's making atonement with the cattle who fast and wear sackcloth (Jonah 3:5-8) and the description of the trial of oxen for goring (*Mishna Sanhedrin* 1:4 on Exodus 21:28-9).

Characteristics of righteousness (*tzadikkim*) that Jews were urged to develop included seeking intimate knowledge of the needs and wants of animals (Proverbs 12:10), saving them in their efforts to preserve the world from natural disaster (Tanhuma, Noah 5), learning how to be kind from shepherding sheep, and compassion in treating camels that demonstrated Rebecca's worthiness as a loyal wife to Isaac (Genesis 24:14-20).

Having compassion for creatures was a particularly important characteristic for a Jew:
"Whoever has compassion upon his fellow creatures, upon him will God have compassion" (ToseftaBavaKamma 9:30; Sifrei Deuteronomy 96).

Compassion, justice, and reciprocity are especially prominent in Christian moral norms for intra-human encounters, but they are less prominent when humans relate to non-human living and inanimate beings.

In hagiography about and by Christian desert fathers, Celtic wanderers, and English hermits can be found expressions of compassion for and reciprocity with animals of all types in diverse natural places.

These holy men variously protected and fed wild animals in their midst, saved them from others' cruelty, showered affection on them, considered some animals their disciples and followers, described animals' reciprocity to them when aiding, feeding, and protecting the holy men that they interpreted as God's ways of providing for them, and depicted animals' lamenting their sicknesses and dying.

Some expressed their deep appreciation for natural settings that prompted them to advocate protecting mountains and plains from destruction. The flowering of their compassion, piety, and sense of reciprocity is exemplified in writings about the life of Francis of Assisi who was proclaimed the patron saint of animals and ecology in 1979 by Pope John Paul II.

When reflecting on Old Testament sources that prohibited cruelty to animals, Aquinas explained that affection and compassion for animals is a characteristic that the faithful should demonstrate and prompt them to be compassionate toward other humans (*Summa theologiae*1 | 2.102.6 ad 8).

Expanding the characteristic of justice to apply directly to non-human living and inanimate creatures remains challenging for Christians to explain theologically today, though their involvement in the Society for the Prevention of Cruelty to Animals and rules proposed by the World Council of Churches to restrict the use of animals for testing products slated for human consumption have been effective.

For Muslims, being just is integral to being conscious of God in every aspect of one's life.

Muslims are called to "stand out firmly for justice, as witnesses to God" and to avoid deviating from justice by constantly revering God who is aware of all we do (*Qur'an* 4:135).

Justice is one of Islam's four core values with loving (*hubb*), humility (*khushu*), and trustworthiness (*amanah*).

Though humans are required to act justly toward one another, especially the poor and vulnerable, as the Prophet Mohammad consistently taught and demonstrated, do Islamic traditions require the faithful to demonstrate justice toward non- human beings?

As a universal law of God, justice should be demonstrated in all aspects of the person's life, and Muslims should never forget that God laid out the earth for many diverse creatures for their use, not solely for human use (*Qur'an* 55:9-10).

A close relationship exists between God, as Lord and Sustainer of the world, and animals that requires us to make and execute decisions that do not disrupt the orderly balance (*mizan*) of the world.

Because humankind was made in a state of goodness with the potential for good actions, we can choose to use our God-bestowed gift to reason from the truth and submit subsequently to God's will in all decisions we make (*Qur'an* 7:181), including decisions that relate to non-human animals and the sustainability of Earth. Muslims are assured that those who act rightly will be rewarded by God (*Qur'an* 2:62).

Principle #6 There are legitimate and illegitimate uses of nature.

Judaic sources and reflections on them affirm this principle absolutely. Some people quote Psalms 115:16 "The heavens belong to the Lord, but the earth He gave over to humanity" as the basis for unbridled human use of God's creation.

However, according to the 12th century Spanish Biblical exegete Abraham ibn Ezra, that interpretation of the psalm is stupid and uninformed:

«The ignorant have compared humanity's rule over the earth with God's rule over the heavens. This is not right, for God rules over everything. The meaning of "but the earth He gave over to humanity" is that humanity is God's steward (*pakeed*) over the earth and must do everything according to God's word».

Humans are not free to do as they please with God's creation.

Ibn Ezra's use of the term *pakeed* is richly suggestive: the root p-k-d has a variety of meanings including command, count, appoint, remember, and deposit.

If humans are the *pakeed*, the agent in whose care a pledge has been placed, the earth is the *pikadon*, the deposit itself, and God is the *mafkeed*, the lessor or depositor.

God also is the *po'kehd*, the one who commands, inspects, and remembers, both for punishment, negative consequences (*po'kehdavon*, "visiting the sin upon"), and for positive ones, including grace (as when God "remembered" Sarah and caused her to conceive).

The notion of stewardship embodies a sense of responsibility in two directions: "downward" for the earth, the deposit, that thing that is held in trust for the sake of the owner, and "upward" to God (*konehshamayimva'aretz*), the creator and possessor of the universe.

Legitimate and illegitimate uses of God's creation pervade Christian sources throughout the centuries. Animals, plants, land, water, and air — the goods of Earth — may be used for the *necessities of life* as the faithful proceed in their temporal lives while hoping for eternal presence before God.

Anything in excess of temporal life's necessities are proscribed; so also are abuse and wastefulness.

As Aquinas and others wrote for their times, God willed into existence a universe in which all components function according to their natures and purposes, but only humans rebel by making and executing decisions that disrupt its functioning through illegitimate uses and actions (e.g., *Summa theologiae* 1.49.3 ad 5, 1|2.109.3; *Compendium theologiae* 192, *Summa contra Gentiles* 3.108.6).

In the New Testament and reflections by theologians, Christians are urged to be vigilant for the return of Jesus the Christ, avoid encumbering themselves with possessions that can choke their desire for God, and orient their temporal lives toward everlasting happiness with God (e.g., Luke 12:32-48, Colossians 3:2).

"The servants of the Lord of Mercy are those who walk gently upon the earth" (*Qur'an* 25:63). How are Muslims urged to walk gently? To share water equitably (*Qur'an* 54:28). To avoid extravagance as urged by the Prophet Muhammad (Sunan Ibn Majah 425). To avoid excessiveness and wastefulness (*Qur'an* 7:31). To not corrupt or upset the balance of nature (*mizan*) God established (*Qur'an* 7:56. 26:151-152, 55:7-8).

Yet our actions have disrupted the balance of creation.

We have managed to change the climate, melt the glaciers at the poles and on mountain-tops, poison rivers, drain lakes, level mountains, corrode the corals in the oceans, poison the soil, denude the forests, and cause the extinction of other species.

Human presence on Earth is short-lived in terms of cosmic time and, as latecomers, we have behaved outrageously.

This geological epoch is now coming to be known as the Anthropocene — a term used to indicate that the human species has now itself become a force of nature.

«Corruption has appeared in both land and sea because of what people's own hands have brought. So that they may taste something of what they have done. So that hopefully they will turn back».

(*Qur'an* 30: 41)

«Thus, Muslims have an ethical imperative and responsibility to maintain and preserve the balance of ecosystems and the biosphere because God "created all things in proportion and measure».

(*Qur'an*: 54:49)

Principle #7: Greed and destructiveness are condemned; restraint and protection are commended.

For Jews, this principle is key and central to the 10th Commandment: "Thou shalt not covet".

Though this commandment reads as an individual precept condemning the coveting of one's neighbor's property, what does "coveting" mean?

An argument among biblical commentators, both Jewish and Christian, for two thousand years has centered around whether this mandate pertains to inner feelings and outward behavior.

Philo, the great Greco-Jewish philosopher of antiquity, generalizes "do not covet" to apply to all forms of covetousness, including greed for money, hunger for honor, sexual lust, hedonism, and gluttony.

He re-emphasizes the emotional states associated with insatiable desires and the importance of spiritual work, which brings us back to the key question of having enough and knowing that it is.

This inner work is a necessary first step towards the ultimate goal of transforming society from its obsession with quantity to striving for quality, from outer acquisition to inner disposition, and from merely having to truly being.

"Who is rich?" one rabbi asked, and answered, "One who is satisfied with one's portion" (PirkeiAvot, *Ethics of the Fathers*, 4:1) should help all pause to think about inner and outward dimensions of coveting.

Maimonides legislated against eating or drinking to excess, wearing ostentatious clothing, or leading an extravagant lifestyle that requires going into debt or living off the largesse of others (*Mishneh Torah, Laws of Opinions* 5).

Let us learn from the wisdom of our tradition.

Greed, destructiveness and wastefulness are among the vices

(bad habits) that Christian sources proscribe, while self-restraint and protection prompted by prudence (informed decision- making) are commended as virtues (good habits) to develop in oneself in order to be inclined to act promptly when seeking and using the goods of Earth.

We should be using them wisely for the necessities of life while assuring their availability to others for their needs.

We should be protecting other species so they can sustain themselves.

We should be protecting the land, waters, and air so they can function according to their natures and provide basic needs for living beings.

Throughout the centuries, Christians have been beseeched to live virtuously — steadfastly prudent, just, moderate, humbly, and compassionately — when relating to and living within this world of many creatures.

We are motivated to live virtuously, Aquinas tells us, for love of our neighbor for whom we wish temporal and eternal happiness and ultimately for love of God whose presence we yearn to enjoy forever (*Summa theologiae*2 | 2.25.2-3; *De caritate*4 and 7).

Muslims who heed the rule "waste not by excess, for God loves not the wasters" (*Qur'an* 7:31) will not waste the goods of Earth. Nor will they be greedy — selfish, excessive in wants with an uncontrolled desire for possessions that denies the same goods to others (*Qur'an* 2:205).

They will not endanger species, destroy their habitats, degrade ecological systems, and threaten the viability of the biosphere because these actions disrupt the order and balance of the universe that God made possible.

Instead, Muslims will honor and embrace their roles as trustees of God's creation by exercising self- restraint when using God's creation, using it for human benefit without causing damage to the other inhabitants of Earth who constitute communities of their own (*Qur'an* 6:38), and protecting its order and balance.

They will "hasten to do good" (*Qur'an* 2:148).

They will take seriously their position as having been appointed by God: "It is God who appointed you as trustees on the Earth" (*Qur'an* 6:165).

They recognize that their Creator "offered the trust to the heavens, the earth and the mountains, but they refused to take it on and shrank from it. But humans took it on" (*Qur'an* 33:72).

Muslims realize the enormity of this trust that imposes on us a moral responsibility — the weightiest of all responsibilities and the price humans pay for the gift of intelligence — the exclusive privilege of communicating and changing the natural world at will. Justice (*adl*) is the basis upon which we are required to execute this trust: "weigh with justice and skimp not in the balance.

God set the earth down for all beings. With its fruits, its palm trees with clustered sheaths" (*Qur'an* 55:7-11).

Muslims will accept, embrace, and demonstrate their sacred duty of trusteeship with a spirit of modesty and altruism by caring for and managing Earth in ways that conform to God's intention.

Principle #8: Humans are obliged to be aware of and responsible for living in harmony with the natural world and should follow the specific practices prescribed by their traditions.

Sources of Judaism accord with this principle that we should be aware of and responsible for living in harmony with the natural world. A range of specific practices can demonstrate this responsibility. According to a 15th century commentary on Deuteronomy 22:6-7:

«The Torah's intention is to prevent the possibility of untimely destruction and to encourage Creation to exist as fully as possible... 'In order that you may fare well and have length of days' means that it shall be good for humankind when Creation is perpetuated so that we will be able to partake of it again in the future...since if we are destined to live for many years on this earth, we are reliant upon Creation perpetuating itself so that we will always have sufficient resources».

(Don Isaac Abravanel, ad loc.)

At the core of this teaching is the covenantal model that establishes an everlasting relationship between God, Israel, and the land of Israel.

This covenant is a subset of a larger God-human (*adam*)-earth (*adamah*) relationship described in the Noahic covenant (Genesis 9:8-17) that includes Earth in its entirety and obliges all inhabitants of our planet to be responsible to God for how we act in relation to Earth.

When underscored, this covenant can be practiced in several ways: by refraining from using labor-saving devices on Shabbat — a day of joy, rest, restoration of strength, and deflation of our arrogance and by avoiding intervention in the creation, thereby limiting human creativity, reinforcing human creatureliness, and demonstrating humility before God as guests responsible for maintaining God's creation (Talmud, Sanhedrin 38).

The accelerated rate of species extinction, degradation of ecological systems, and threats to the viability of Earth's biosphere warrant our following this principle in the Middle East, North Africa, and all over the world.

Since 1983, the World Council of Churches has been encouraging Christians to make justice, peace, and the integrity of Creation central to our lives.

Popes John Paul II and Benedict XVI issued statements in 1990 and 2010 linking our moral responsibility for living in harmony with Earth and one another.

Pope Francis and Patriarch Bartholomew have been vigorously urging Christians and others to be aware of their responsibilities for Earth, the home we share with one another, other species, their habitats, and ecological systems.

All Christian denominations have been invited to reflect on our moral responsibilities to care about and for Earth on *The World Day of Prayer for the Care of Creation* that is celebrated annually on September 1.

Though this day provides an important reminder for Christians to express our gratitude to God for our common home and to demonstrate our gratitude through words and actions, one day a year is inadequate for addressing the many threats to the Earth community.

Plans are underway through the Vatican's Dicastery for Promoting Integral Human Development for a multi-faceted commemoration of Pope Francis's epochal 2015 encyclical throughout 2020 during which parishes, dioceses, educational institutions, and non-government organizations will be asked to take the *Laudato si'* Pledge to pray for and with creation, live more simply, and advocate protection of our common home at all levels of governance.

More faith-based actions are needed to mitigate the effects of human-forced climate change and other environmental problems that inevitably have social ramifications — especially for poor and vulnerable people.

According to the *Qur'an*, "Corruption has appeared on land and sea because of what the hands of humans have wrought, that God may make them taste a part of that which they have done, in order that they may return [to guidance]" (30:41).

Returning to the sources of Islam — the *Qur'an* and the Sunnah — that tell Muslims about God's creation, our place in the natural order, and the responsibilities we must shoulder as trustees.

We need to regain that consciousness we once had of the oneness of God's creation, that we are deeply and irrevocably interwoven into its fabric, that we are causing grievous bodily harm to God's creation, and that harm is hurting us.

Now is the time for a reappraisal of our core sources through which to gain a fresh and meaningful understanding of what they are telling and guiding us about living responsibly in the world as true trustees.

The *Qur'an* describes the Prophet Muhammad as having been "endowed with a noble character" (*Qur'an* 68:4) and reminds us that "in the Messenger of God you have a beautiful pattern of conduct" (*Qur'an* 33:21).

He is a role model for living in harmony with the natural world.

His attitudes toward nature and animals are concrete examples for us as manifestations of the *Qur'anic* spirit.

He attached great importance in his own practice and sayings (*hadiths*) not only to public worship, civil law, and social etiquette, but also to planting trees, preserving forests, conserving the environment, and compassionately treating animals.

He is the exemplar for us to recognize and emulate through our actions today.

Bibliography and Further Readings

Ali, Y. (1983), *The Holy Qur'an*, Trns. Yusuf Ali, Maryland: Amana Corp.
Canan I. (1982), *Kutub-u Sitte* (Turkish trans.), Istanbul.
Asad, M. (1980), *The Message of The Qur'ān*, Dar al-Andalus: Gibraltar, 1980.
Chittick, W. (1986), *God Surrounds All Things: An Islamic Perspective on the Environment. The World and I*, vol.I, no.6, June.
Diamond, J. (2005), *Collapse: How Societies Choose to Fail or Succeed*, Viking Penguin.
... (1997), *Guns, Germs and Steel*, Viking Penguin.
Elmandjra, M. (1990), *The Future of the Islamic World*, A paper presented in the Symposium on *The Future of the Islamic World*, Algiers.
Husaini W. A. (1980), *Islamic Environmental Systems Engineering*, Macmillan Press, London.
Iqbal Sir Mohammad, *The Reconstruction of Religious Thought in Islam*, (Lahore: The Ashraf Press, 1958).
Izz b. Abdisselam (1980), *Kavaidu'l-Ahkam fi Mesalihi'l-Enam*, Beyrut: Daru'l- Ceyl.
IzziDeen, Mawil Y. (Samarrai),(1990), *Islamic Environmental Ethics, Law, and Society*, in Ed. J. Ronald.
Engel ve Joan Gibb Engel, *Ethics of Environment and Development. Global Challenge, International Response*, London: Belhaver Press.
Khalid F. and O'Brien, J. (ed.), (1992), *Islam and Ecology*, New York: Cassell Publishers Limited.
Khalid, F. (2019), *Signs on the Earth: Islam, Modernity and the Climate Crisis* (Markleld, UK: Kube).
Lamartine A. (1857), *History Of Turkey*, D. Appleton & Company, New York.
Lane, E. (2014), *Manners and Customs of the Modern Egyptians*,

American University in Cairo Press, Beirut.
Manzoor S. P. (1984), *Environment and Values: the Islamic Perspective*, in *The Touch of Midas: Science, values and environment in Islam and the West*, ed., ZiauddinSardar, Manchester University Press.
Matin Ibrahim Abdul (2012), *Green Deen; What Islam Teaches about Protecting the Planet*, Kube Publishing Ltd, UK.
Nasif A. O. (1987), *The Muslim Declaration of Nature*, *Environmental Policy and Law*, 17/1.
Nasr S. H. (1997), *.Man and Nature*, (Chicago: Kazi Publications, 1997).
... (1992), *Islam and the Environmental Crisis*, in *Spirit of Nature*, (edts) Steven C. Rockefeller and John C. Elder, (Boston): Beacon Prass, 1992.
Nicholson, R. (1975), *The Mystics of Islam*, London: Routledge and Kegan Paul.
Mardin S.(1989), *Religion and Social Change in Modern Turkey, The Case of Bediuzzaman Said Nursi* , Albany: SUNY Press.
Nursî B. S. (1995), *The Flashes*, trans. SukranVahide, Istanbul: Sözler Publications.
... (1998), *The Words*, trans. SukranVahide, Istanbul: Sözler Publications, new ed.
... (1999), *Epitomes of Light, (Mathnawi al-Nuriya), The Essentials of Risale-i Nur*, trans: A.Unal, Izmir: Kaynak.
Özdemir İ. (2003), *Said Nursi*, in *Encyclopedia of Religion and Nature*, ed. Bron Taylor and Jeffrey Kaplan (New York: Continuum, 2003).
... (2007), *The Ethical Dimension of Human Attitude Towards Nature*, (Istanbul: InsanYayinlari).
... (2017), *Muhammad Iqbal and Environmental Ethics*, *Acta Via Serica*, Vol. 2, No. 2,, pp. 87-110.
... (2003), *Towards an Understanding of Environmental Ethic from A Qur'anic Perspective, Islam and Ecology*, Ed. Richard Foltz(Harvard University Press), pp. 1-37.

Rumi J. (1977), *The Mathnawi of Jalalu'ddin Rumi*, trans. R.A. Nicholson, London: Luzac.

... (2000) *Divan-iKebîr*, trans. Nevit O. Ergin, Los Angels: Echo Publications.

Vahide S. (2005), *Islam in Modern Turkey: An Intellectual Biography of Bediuzzaman Said Nursi*, State University of New York Press.